PRAISE FOR SOUL STRENGTH

"I have known Dr. Alan Ahlgrim for decades. It's hard to express my joy at seeing his wisdom and expertise captured on the written page. This is not a feel-good book filled with fluff. What you'll find instead is pure gold forged and refined over a lifetime into practical insight for change from the inside out."

—*Dr. John Walker*
Founder of Blessing Ranch Ministry
Co-author of Unhindered: Aligning
the Story of Your Heart

"The best teachers are lifelong learners, and Alan is definitely that. In *Soul Strength* Alan shares his life experiences and encounters with transformation. *Soul Strength* is inspiring, enlightening, and full of practical wisdom. Take your time with it—and invite others to join you on the journey!"

—*Bob Hudson*
Founder of Men at the Cross
www.menatthecross.com

"This book is a treasure! As a participant in two covenant groups led by my friend and mentor Alan Ahlgrim, I have been blessed to have experienced the power of these twelve principles firsthand. In *Soul Strength*, Alan has consolidated life-changing wisdom, experiences, and stories from decades of ministry into a well-written, funny, and practical tool. If you care about your soul, read this book!"

—*Arron Chambers*
Pastor and Life/Marriage/Business Coach
Author of Eats with Sinners: Loving Like Jesus

"Alan is both my friend and my ministry yokefellow in the cause of energizing and equipping twenty-first-century church leaders. He excels as a pastor to pastors, with his rare relational savvy and communication giftedness as a counselor, teacher, and writer. As someone who has personally benefited greatly from Alan's 'soul care' initiative through the years, I encourage everyone looking to advance their life's purpose to read this book."

—*Ken Idleman*
VP of Leadership Development
for the Solomon Foundation

"As someone who has spiritually benefited from the transparency and accountability of active participation in a men's group, I am grateful for Alan's vision and labor to produce this high-quality practical resource for deeper discipleship."

—*Kyle Idleman*
Lead Pastor of Southeast Christian Church
Author of Not a Fan

"Alan Ahlgrim has captured twelve empowering principles that will help you remain faithful despite the highs and lows of ministry and life. What Alan shares isn't talked about or taught in seminary, which is why *Soul Strength* is a must-read for anyone preparing for pastoral ministry. As a recipient of his insightful teaching and coaching, I can tell you that this book has the potential to enrich your life."

—*Clark Tanner*
Northwest Executive Director
of PastorServe

"I didn't want to stop reading! In *Soul Strength* there is something positive and applicable for every leader or pastor in whatever season they are in."

—*Dr. Don Wilson*
Accelerate Group

"I will be quoting this material for many decades! *Soul Strength* is not just inspirational, it's transformational! Filled with high-powered challenges to get you out of your head and into the deeper aspects of life and spirituality, *Soul Strength* will bring out the best in you. Buckle up and get ready to be changed for the better and forever."

—*Dr. Charity Byers*
Blessing Ranch Ministries
Co-author of Unhindered: Aligning
the Story of Your Heart

"*Soul Strength* is a gold mine filled with a lifetime of wisdom on how you can lead yourself and others toward a deeply transformed life. After being mentored by Alan and following the principles in this book, my personal and professional relationships have never been deeper or more satisfying than they are today. If you are looking for a more impactful life, this is your roadmap!"

—*Shan Moyers*
Lead Pastor of Rocky Mountain Christian Church

"*Soul Strength* is a premium guide to making the most of the life that God has given you. As a psychologist who specializes in the mental health of ministry leaders, I know that Dr. Ahlgrim's insight is desperately needed. Many leaders will save themselves a world of hurt and experience greater ministry wellbeing by reading and metabolizing *Soul Strength*."

—*Dr. Wes Beavis, Clinical Psychologist*
Author of Let's Talk About Ministry Burnout

"I am the beneficiary of Alan's mentorship before this book, and I am so glad he wrote this stuff down! This is an incredibly thoughtful compilation of principles that only a sensei like Alan could pull together. Alan really did his homework on this one. *Soul Strength* is a book you'll want to keep close at hand as you move through your life."

—*Dr. Tim Harlow*
Lead Pastor, Parkview Christian Church
Author of Life on Mission *and*
What Made Jesus Mad

"Alan Ahlgrim has an uncanny way of getting you to let down your guard, all while sneaking up on you with an incredible Spirit-filled truth. *Soul Strength* will take you to that place over and over again! Let these principles wash over you and get in the cracks of a thirsty heart!"

—*Jerry Harris*
Senior Pastor of The Crossing/Multisite

"If you've ever longed for soul-strengthening relationships, *Soul Strength* is for you. As a psychologist, I've read many books about how to deepen friendships. This, by far, is my favorite. It will show you exactly how to form a small group of fellow journeyers who will sustain you and help you to grow in new ways."

—*Dr. Jay Lindsay*
Psychologist

"*Soul Strength: Rhythms for Thriving* is a gift to the church! Who doesn't long to thrive? I know I do—and not only for my good but for the good of others. I was reading this book on a recent flight and was reminded before takeoff that in case of an emergency when the oxygen masks drop from the ceiling, we are to put our masks on before seeking to help others. This book by Dr. Alan Ahlgrim is an oxygen mask for our souls! It's practical and timely—and will equip you to help others. Thank you, Alan!"

—*Eric Most*
Vice President, Rocky Mountain Region
National Christian Foundation

"My friend Alan Ahlgrim has been a personal coach and mentor for over thirty years. He has helped me remain Christ focused and spiritually balanced throughout my career as a county sheriff. Through some really difficult periods Alan has helped keep me centered. I believe this book will bless many, many people with Alan's rich insights."

—*Sheriff Joe Pelle*
Boulder County, Colorado

"I know no one who has been more intentional about developing soul-health than Alan. And I know no one who has been more invested in helping others develop the same vital, life-giving trait. You want to read Alan's book!"

—*Eddie Lowen*
Lead Pastor of West Side
Christian Church

"Alan Ahlgrim shares from his heart the critical need for soul care for everyone who heeds the call to serve God. Read this and learn from one of the best!"

—*Matthew LaGrange, PhD*
Founder and Executive Director of
His Story Coaching and Counseling

"While serving as president of the National Christian Foundation Colorado, I met no other pastor as committed as Alan Ahlgrim to living a life of extravagant generosity and—even more importantly—using his time, talent, and treasure to encourage his congregation to do the same. After I heard about Alan's 90 Day Tithing Challenge—with a money-back guarantee!—from members of his congregation who didn't want to stop double tithing because God had blessed them so abundantly, I began sharing his story with every pastor I met. If every pastor was as bold and courageous as Alan Ahlgrim, how much would the needle of generosity increase? How much more joy would people in their congregations experience from living a life of extravagant generosity?"

—*Bryan Chrisman*
Senior Advisor of The Impact Foundation

"High praise and congratulations to Alan Ahlgrim for *Soul Strength!* After decades of faithful and Spirit-led ministry shepherding congregations, Pastor Ahlgrim offers practical, biblically based tools to inspire, guide, and fuel Christ-centered, heartfelt leadership. Whatever your calling, *Soul Strength* will help you embrace your God-ordained assignment and live a summoned life full of gratitude for God's ultimate gift: His son, Jesus Christ."

—*Kathryn Hopping*
Attorney-at-Law

"As I am learning to relax in the sovereignty of God, I've come to realize that we are far from alone in our journey of the soul. Alan's reflection and articulation of real soul pain, which somehow, always leads to real soul joy, breathes life through these pages."

—*Dr. Jay Scott*
Pastor of Worthington
Christian Church

"After twenty years in vocational ministry and a season of near burnout along the way, I was thrilled to experience the content and ideas found in this book, and I can't wait to share it with everyone."

—*Ross Runnels*
Pastor of Canoe Creek
Christian Church

"Having participated in one of Alan's soul care groups, I have seen his twelve transcendent principles in action, and benefitted personally from the power of their Spirit-directed, biblical truth. Now, part of my mission is to continue practicing these rhythms for thriving and pass them along to all who have ears to hear. Thank you, Alan, for this excellent kingdom resource!"

—*Dr. Rick Grover*
Lead Pastor of East 91st Street
Christian Church

"For more than two decades Alan has been a wise advisor in my life. Then I had the privilege of participating in a soul care covenant group that he led. He not only helped me to see the value of heart-sharing over 'shop talk,' he also challenged me to understand that finishing well is being 'more in love with Jesus at the end than the beginning.' These are just two of the many soul-enriching principles he explores in this helpful book."

—*Dr. Clay Peck*
Lead Pastor of Grace Place
Author of The Main Thing

"Alan's years of experience connecting people at a heart level come together in the pages of his book in an easily understandable and readily applicable way. Thanks to *Soul Strength*, these kinds of heart connections are accessible to anyone who will simply take the time to read and apply the principles of this very insightful and helpful book."

—*Bryan Myers*
Academy Christian Church

"I walked somewhat cautiously into the first session of my covenant group with Alan. It was an experience that I have relished. Today, I am so grateful that I said yes. May your experience abound with gratitude as well."

—*Steve Larson*
Pastor of Community
Celebration Church

"What Alan shares with us in this book is what I have experienced with him in life. My three-year journey in my covenant group has been the most enriching for me as a child of God, a husband, a father, and a pastor. The lack of real community starves the soul. Going small, going strong, going slow is the Jesus way of soul nourishment."

—*John "Didi" Bacon*
Senior Minister of Mount
Carmel Christian Church

"Alan Ahlgrim knows transformation. He's experienced it himself as God has grown him through years of fruitful yet challenging ministry. Transformation leaves scars, and Alan isn't afraid to discuss them openly and honestly. He's also been leading men through transformation in his soul care groups for years. To spend time with Alan, whether in person or by adopting the practices in this book, is to submit yourself to a great shaping. And it is a shaping that you won't regret."

—Nick Vipperman
Senior Minister of Galilee
Christian Church

"Scripture is clear that personal transformation happens best in Christ-centered relationships. Dr. Alan Ahlgrim does a masterful job defining the kinds of people, experiences, places, conversations, and content that enable transformation to be a reality. I highly recommend this book!"

—Tim Wallingford, D. Min.
Executive Director of The Christian
Church Leadership Network

"While *Soul Strength* is life-changing for any Christian, it is a must-read for anyone in church leadership. Dr. Ahlgrim's experience as a pastor and mentor shines forth in this practical and engaging book. As you finish the last page, you'll be encouraged and excited to take the steps necessary to be able to say with authenticity, 'It is well with my soul.'"

—*Andy Rodriguez*
Vice President of Mustard Seed Network
Pastor of Mustard Seed Christian Church

"*Soul Strength* is the antidote to our toxic 'I demand results now!' culture. After learning the hard way that church programs don't produce transformation, Alan Ahlgrim shows us how to follow Jesus' model. The result? Soul-strengthening communities of people who, over time, grow more honest, more reflective, more purposeful, more fulfilled."

—*Dr. LeRoy Lawson*
Retired minister and college president

"Dr Alan Ahlgrim has tackled a big topic within the church world today: What pastors and church leaders need to know about the sensitive subject of soul care. His twelve principles will change your thought process. A must read for all pastors!"

—*Douglas J. Crozier*
Chief Executive Officer of the
Solomon Foundation

"Hebrews 13:7 (ESV) says 'Remember your leaders, those who spoke to you the word of God. Consider the outcome of their way of life and imitate their faith.' This describes Alan. His life, leadership, and ministry are worth considering, and his faith is absolutely worth imitating. If you have not had the privilege of spending time with Alan and gleaning from his incredible wisdom and care, this book is a gift to you. If you want depth and joy in relationships, or are looking for transformation in your life, get ready to learn from one of the best."

—*Matt Hessel*
Lead Pastor of LifeBridge
Christian Church

"*Soul Strength* provides practical steps to develop meaningful relationships beyond the superficial encounters we commonly and inappropriately call 'relationships.' Dr. Ahlgrim's twelve transcendent principles are not complicated, and the result—being a member of a soul enriching covenant group—is an investment that will enrich your life for the rest of your life."

—*Rick Parker*
Corporate HR director, retired

"This book could make a huge difference on the quality of your life. Alan's experience and amazing way with words capture simple but powerful truths that have guided me and others toward a lasting resiliency. If you're ready to go from surviving to thriving, don't just read the book, engage with both the book and the workbook with trusted friends. It's so worth it."

—*Glen Elliott*
Lead Pastor of Pantano
Christian Church

"There are thousands of books about strengthening your financial life, your love life, and your physical life. Unfortunately, not many have been devoted to strengthening what matters most—your soul. Proverbs 4:7 (NIV) says, 'Get wisdom. Though it cost all you have, get understanding.' Alan Ahlgrim has spent his life getting wisdom on how to care for your own soul and the souls of others, and he has put the best of it in this book. Get this book, and you will get the best of his godly wisdom."

—*Brian Mavis*
President of America's Kids Belong

"In a time and climate when many are looking for hope and encouragement, Alan Ahlgrim's book *Soul Strength* offers both! If you ready to go deeper in your walk with the Lord, get this book!"

—*Joe Herzanek*
President of Changing Lives Foundation
Author of Why Don't They Just Quit

"Alan Ahlgrim has earned the right to speak authoritatively about 'soul strength.' He successfully led a dynamic, healthy church. He then navigated the ship through some turbulent waters and yet survived and continues to thrive. Most importantly, he genuinely loves other church leaders. His counsel will help you stay spiritually healthy while nurturing and shepherding others."

—*Bob Russell*
Author of Transition Plan, After 50 Years of Ministry,
When God Builds a Church

"When our ministry at CFR has looked for an expert to help our partner pastors on soul care and soul strength we have turned to Alan Alghrim. In this book you will learn timeless truths to help you strengthen your soul."

—*Darren Key, CFP*
Chief Executive Officer of
Christian Financial Resources, Inc.

SOUL
STRENGTH

SOUL
STRENGTH

RHYTHMS FOR THRIVING

DR. ALAN AHLGRIM

12 TRANSCENDENT PRINCIPLES

ILLUMIFY
MEDIA.COM

SOUL
STRENGTH

The views and opinions expressed in this book are those of the author and do not necessarily reflect the official policy or position of Illumify Media Global.

Published by
Illumify Media Global
www.IllumifyMedia.com
"Let's bring your book to life!"

Library of Congress Control Number: 2021922600

Paperback ISBN: 978-1-955043-36-6

Typeset by Art Innovations (http://artinnovations.in/)
Cover design by Debbie Lewis

Printed in the United States of America

To Linda, my devoted wife... for life!

You are the wisest, strongest, most calming and enriching person in my world. You are my irreplaceable partner in all things, without whom I would never have experienced the blessing of family, and so much joyful fulfillment and wellness of soul.

"There are many virtuous and capable women in the world, but you surpass them all."

(Proverbs 31:29)

CONTENTS

ACKNOWLEDGMENTS

There are indeed, as Hebrews 12:1 (NIV) says, "a great cloud of witnesses" surrounding me as I have been preparing this resource for life and leadership. Certainly, this includes all those faithful partners in the churches I have served and the loyal allies among the fraternity of pastors and leaders who have enlightened and encouraged me for decades. They are my true heroes in whom I take great delight! (Psalm 16:3).

Even though I do not have space to name the many dozens in this category, these four merit special acknowledgment:

First, my friend of fifty years, Cam Huxford. As Paul said of Timothy in Philippians 2:22 (MSG), "I have no one quite like [him]."

Second, Dr. John Walker, my heart-shaping partner for decades through what he calls "the practice of intentional collegiality." "He is my partner who works with me to help you" (2 Corinthians 8:23).

Third, Shan Moyers, my successor in ministry at Rocky Mountain Christian Church, as we have sought to outdo the other in showing honor (Romans 12:10 ESV).

Finally, Steve and Celeste Yager, two of our most generous and faithful friends who have been the wind beneath the wings of this book with uncommon encouragement. "I want you to receive a reward for your kindness" (Philippians 4:17).

FOREWORD

A couple years ago, after an extended time of fasting and praying for God's vision for my next run of church leadership, an audacious kingdom goal snapped into focus for me: disciple one thousand men!

I had been asking God for fresh vision for the growth of our church, but apparently He had a different idea—one that was far more personal and intimate. The vision He gave me wasn't for the leadership or the members of our church but for *me*. He gave me a vision of personal impact.

He told me to disciple one thousand men.

I was dumbstruck at first. How do you get started on a project like that? After all, Jesus discipled twelve men, and it took Him three years to do it.

Before long, I began to get excited about the impact such a goal might have. Jesus' disciples embraced His strategy and turned the world upside down.

Why is discipleship such a game-changer? How do we even start? What kind of person does God empower to pull this off? How are we changed in the process?

Fortunately, my friend Alan Ahlgrim answers these questions and more in the pages of this book. In fact, he has written a play book that you and I can use to build spiritually strong relationships over the long haul—and equip others do the same.

In other words, by embracing the principles Alan walks us through in the pages of his book, we can have access to the profound process that Jesus used to transform the lives of the people He loved.

This process is not fast. Jesus showed us there is no fast way to build the kind of life-giving relationships that have the power to change not only our lives but the lives of others.

There is, however, a path we can take.

And Alan knows the way.

My life is proof that the principles Alan shares in this book really work. We have enjoyed a fifty-year friendship that started when he was a young church planter, and I was a fifteen-year-old from a single-parent home attending youth camp.

Over the years, Alan used the principles found in this book to mentor and encourage me in life-changing ways. Like "iron sharpens iron," we have sharpened each other for five decades! I cannot imagine what my life would be like without the catalytic friendship we've enjoyed.

In this book Alan shares his secret so others can create the kind of encouraging, empowering, sustaining connection he and I have enjoyed over the years.

If you implement what you read here, you'll be next.

Alan writes this book from a unique well of wisdom and experience. He has implemented these principles as the pastor of a church plant that became a fast-growing megachurch. Today, he's coaching hundreds of pastors and church members to embrace these principles in Covenant groups—small, committed communities in which deep connections thrive.

My hope is that as you read this book, you'll be inspired to form your own Covenant Group with which to journey through these chapters. (To learn how, visit covenantconnections.life.)

As Alan says, your life is only as rich as your relationships. I encourage you to share this book, re-read it yourself every year, and get to work.

I want everyone I mentor to read this book!

T. Cam Huxford
Senior Pastor of
Compassion Christian Church,
Savannah, Georgia

INTRODUCTION: START HERE!

"TWO ARE BETTER THAN ONE, BECAUSE THEY HAVE
A GOOD RETURN FOR THEIR WORK: IF EITHER OF
THEM FALLS DOWN, ONE CAN HELP THE OTHER UP.
BUT PITY ANYONE WHO FALLS AND HAS NO ONE TO
HELP HIM UP."

—ECCLESIASTES 4:9-10 NIV

This book may not change your life . . . but it could! While some may casually read this and get some benefit, others will settle in with it, assimilate it, and never be the same.

Those who have gone before you have found the soul-enriching contents of this book to be catalytic when processed in deep community. Everything that follows has been a soul-refreshing resource propelling others to new levels of peace, purpose, and fulfillment. The same could be true for you. You could discover soul-filling abundance, the blessing of multidimensional thriving!

In a time when many are merely surviving, those who embrace a deeper life will begin to thrive. So, if you yearn to move beyond a life of drudgery to a life of high calling, from soul-crushing isolation to vigorous community, this is for you. Consider the life-giving rhythms described and presented in this book to be God's gift to you!

Whether you are an established church leader or a brand-new believer, there are twelve transcendent principles that have the power to enrich and transform your life. When you embrace these principles, you make space for your soul to flourish, creating the kind of growth and transformation you long for.

Soul care isn't selfish. Investing in yourself is a good thing. Investing in yourself empowers you to invest in others. When your soul is thriving, you are in a healthier place to connect with yourself, with others, and with God.

You may have explored many methods of soul care in the past. That's good.

But there is something more.

And it is the key to . . . well, everything.

CRACKING THE CODE OF TRANSFORMATIVE SOUL CARE

I've been trying to crack the code of transformative soul care for decades. Clearly, transformation is not a destination but a journey. And that journey cannot be undertaken alone.

The missing element in spiritual transformation for many—even for many in Christian leadership—is life with the right people. We all need to encircle ourselves with a core of healthy others who are actively seeking the best, both for themselves and for us! Both are vital. Many say that they want the best, but their lives give no evidence of seeking the best, which doesn't happen easily or automatically. We all need partners in pursuing soul strength.

Here's what doing life with the right people can do for us:

- Help us move from casual interactions to in-depth relationship.
- Help us move from head land to heart land.
- Help us move from "just another interesting study" to regular "aha" moments.
- Help us move from endless sports talk or shop talk to life-on-life soul talk.

Tending to your soul in partnership with others was a practice established from the very beginning of creation.

God said from the very start, "It's not good for man to be alone" (see Genesis 2:18).

I used to think this statement from Genesis 2 applied only to men needing marriage. Clearly, that's true for most men, and most women as well, but that's not all. Every one of us was built for community. We were hardwired to connect with both our heads and our hearts. Together is better!

Let me tell you about a television series called *Alone* that I stumbled across. Ten determined survivalists were each deposited in different parts of the Vancouver Island wilderness in late fall, early winter. The challenge was to see just who would last the longest alone. The grand prize was $500,000!

These were trained and experienced wilderness experts. They were each allowed to select ten items for survival. Things like knives, tarps, fishing line, cooking pots, and axes. In addition, they were issued essentials such as a medical kit, bear spray, flares, and satellite phones for emergency rescue. One tough guy lasted only one night because of the bears that terrified him prowling around his tent. Another tapped out from drinking contaminated water. Most lasted several weeks. Only two lasted more than seven weeks. They were gaunt, cold, and lonely to the point of tears.

The loneliness-driven tears surprised me the most. Participants had been encouraged to spill their guts before the cameras, and they did just that . . . even to the point of grieving with heaving over being separated from family and friends.

These tough guys didn't just *feel* alone; they really were alone. Each was separated from the others by miles, with no means of communication, and it nearly drove them crazy. One of them said, "I'm not good in the head."

Life alone is a miserable life.

In his book *We Need to Hang Out*, Billy Baker shares insights from his research on loneliness.

Baker quotes Drs. Richard Schwartz and Jacqueline Olds, authors of *The Lonely American: Drifting Apart in the Twenty-first Century*, who wrote: "Psychiatry has worked hard to destigmatize things like depression, and to a large part it has been successful. People are comfortable saying they're depressed. But they're not comfortable saying they're lonely, because you're the kid sitting alone in the cafeteria."

Billy Baker confesses that, after completing his research on loneliness, "I had to admit that I had no truly active friendships."

Sadly, that's how many leaders feel. While they may have professional or even pastoral relationships with many, they have personal relationships with very few. Some have in-depth relationships with no one!

When I've been asked about the heart condition of leaders these days, I sum it up like this:

- They're running scared—constantly chasing the call to be relevant.
- They're running on fumes—living with a weariness of soul that a good night's sleep won't cure.
- They're running alone—feeling like no one really knows them at their core.

As a leader myself, I have had personal experience with all three! During one of the times of struggle during my ministry, I was on the scary brink of emotional exhaustion. As I shared my soul depletion with my wife, Linda, she strongly challenged me by saying, "It can't be God's will for you to be doing everything you are doing if you're feeling the way you are feeling!" My wife doesn't have the mercy gift; she has the wisdom gift. That was a catalytic comment. The changes didn't all come overnight, but they did begin that night. I knew that I needed to get some help from some healthy others.

Your life and mine will never be any richer than our relationships! I don't need to spend seven weeks alone, shivering in the wet cold and surviving on seaweed and slugs, to convince me of that.

I am deeply grateful for the rich relationships God has provided for me.

Do you have a growing number of life-giving relationships?

MAKING LIFE UP AS YOU GO? WELCOME TO THE CLUB

Over the five decades of my ministry, I have often been desperate for God's help. When we were starting a new church in South Carolina, I felt anxious, uncertain, and entirely alone. Frankly, I didn't really know what I was doing.

Then, as I gradually began to share my confusion with others in leadership, I discovered that my struggles weren't unique to me. Others were typically as clueless and overwhelmed as I was. Making that discovery left me both surprised and gratified!

Everyone shares something in common with Indiana Jones in the classic movie *Raiders of the Lost Ark*. You probably remember the scene. He and a few of his confused allies were surrounded by the enemy, and all hope seemed lost.

When asked how he was possibly going to catch the bad guys rapidly driving a truck away on a desert road, he quickly said, "I don't know. I'm making this up as I go!"

Truth be told, we are all making life up day by day, week by week, and scene by scene. Unfortunately, we usually think we're the only ones doing that. Only when we get honest with others do we discover that we're not alone after all. The Christian life is never a solo affair. We all need to know that's it's safe to share our headaches and heartaches. In fact, as we do, we discover resources and rich relationships we never dreamed existed for us.

My big, compelling, lifelong craving has been for deep connection with others. It's what led me to reach out to connect in my early days of ministry and what drives me still. Our enemy wants to isolate us. God wants to connect us.

I became involved leading small groups in my thirties. In the ensuing decades, I've led a wide variety of groups, seminars, and workshops. I've shared this message on the big stage and in small settings.

Most leaders define influence as "big." Our culture admires going big, going fast—but inevitably that means going shallow. The truth is, if I had a choice between speaking to five thousand people on relational stuff or spending five days with five guys and going deep, everyone who knows me knows what I would pick. We can only go deeper with fewer.

HOW TO GET THE MOST FROM THIS BOOK

There are three ways to journey through this book. You will benefit from all three. But I'll be honest with you: One approach is good. The second is better. And the third approach I'm going to tell you about is the best.

This is good:

Journey through these twelve transcendent principles on your own. You'll find questions for reflection throughout the chapters. I encourage you to keep a journal, writing your answers to questions and journaling about insights you may receive. There is a companion journal to this book, with additional questions and features that will make the journey more impactful for you. You can download a sample of the journal or purchase the full journal at covenantconnections.life/journal.

This is better:

Journey through these chapters with one or more friends.

After all, community is catalytic, and candor is a growth accelerator!

It's been said that everything big begins with a conversation. This I know: Some of the best conversations have yet to be started. Some of the best friendships have yet to be formed. Some of the best experiences may just be ready to unfold.

I encourage you to invite a few others to join you in reading this book and embarking on a journey to discover a soul-enriching community of deep connection. Think of it as a small circle of soul care.

- Ask God to prompt you to think of a few to invite into this adventure.

- Suggest a predictable rhythm, i.e., weekly, biweekly or monthly.

- Encourage everyone to read one chapter and to ponder a few of the questions for that chapter, in advance of each meeting.

- Download a sample of the companion journal or purchase the full journal at covenantconnections. life/journal

- Take notes as you read. We all remember better what we write.

- Share with each other what you are learning from God—that's applied theology!

This is best:

The deepest transformation communities I've seen have been in covenant groups. These intentional groups put spiritual growth on steroids!

Covenant groups are designed to provide a safe and confidential setting in which to process life, a healthy community in which members are committed to helping one another serve and finish well.

Covenant groups are not couples' groups or a mix of both men and women. Rarely do men go deep in the presence of women. I'm told the same is true for women in the presence of men.

I have been leading these kinds of groups for several decades. Why do they make such a difference? Covenant groups create intentional, disciplined community. That's the secret sauce. Covenant groups are calendared. They are prioritized.

Everyone needs a track to run on, and a team to run with. Covenant groups provide both. To learn more about journeying through these chapters with others in your own Covenant group, visit: covenantconnections.life.

All of us need to know that another human being not only cares about us but also understands us. Better still, we all need a safe place to share our struggles honestly. Not just to *go through* life and leadership but to *grow through* life and leadership. Together!

My most compelling motivation is to provide an avenue for soul-enriching group life. We all need people to call us up (not out) to something better. My encore role now not only involves connecting with leaders but helping leaders connect.

Soul strength is contagious; we catch it from those in deep community with us. What you hold in your hands right now is not just another resource to casually scan and soon set aside. This is intended to be your companion in a soul-strengthening journey, a catalyst for deeper relationships than you may ever have enjoyed before.

My purpose in writing this book is that it would find its way not merely to your shelf but into your life! You don't need another book; you need a revitalizing and transformational experience. That will only happen through soul-enriching conversations in a close community. Everyone needs a relational oasis.

So, who might you know that could join you on a soul-strengthening journey? You just need a few others, maybe even just one. The key will be a mutual desire not just to survive in life and leadership but to thrive!

Life is messy, but it doesn't have to be lonely, so buckle up and let's begin . . . together!

Grace and peace,

Dr. Alan Ahlgrim
Founder and CSO (Chief Soul Care Officer)
Covenantconnections.life

CHAPTER 1

EMBRACE YOUR STORY

"GRANT, LORD, THAT I MAY KNOW MYSELF
THAT I MAY KNOW THEE."

—AUGUSTINE

After sharing his heartbreaking story, Doug added, "I'm fifty-four, and I've never felt that I belonged until now."

The more Doug and others shared in depth, the more everyone felt connected. Seven men became a band of brothers at that retreat.

The stories I hear that mean the most are the ones that have been thoroughly processed and owned. They are the ones that spring from the heart and not just the head. I'm learning that the stories that are the most personal are indeed the most universal.

Oswald Chambers says, "If you are not diligent and say, 'I'm not going to study and struggle to express this truth in my own words; I'll just borrow my words from someone else,' then the words will be of no value to you or to others. . . . Your position is not really yours until you make it yours through suffering and study."[1]

It's been said that nothing is more dangerous than "trafficking in unfelt truth."[2] I know. Early in my ministry, feeling stressed, I borrowed a sermon title and more without giving any credit at all. After the service the oldest member of our tiny church greeted me at the door and said, "I've always appreciated the messages of Peter Marshall."

Ouch!

While no one has a monopoly on truth and we all need to lean on others and learn from each other, the stories we tell that we truly own—because they *are* our own—will always have the greatest impact.

In other words, when you have personally struggled with tough stuff, don't be afraid to own it and share it with others.

We don't want another entertaining talk. Everyone is weary of words. We are all inundated with information. Great books, blogs, and podcasts abound. We're gluttons when it comes to content, but we're starving for heartfelt truth and in-depth conversation.

By now we should all know that Twitter does not produce transformation! Rather, we're all in desperate need of knowing that we're not alone in the journey of life. And we all have a true story to tell.

STRUGGLES ARE OUR TRAINING GROUND

One of my close pastor friends is struggling right now to find the strength to lead well. He is a tough guy but has grown soul weary. Like many, he candidly admits to having been *going through*, not *growing through*, the current COVID-19 crisis.

He is not alone.

More pastors than ever are wondering not simply how they'll come up with yet another strong sermon but where they will find the strength to proclaim it. They are riddled with anxiety and sometimes literally unable to catch their breath in front of a congregation. I personally know how hard it is to speak when you can barely breathe!

Years ago Boulder Police Officer Beth Haynes was killed in the line of duty. When I was asked to lead the memorial service, I was both highly honored and highly anxious. On the day of the service thousands of uniformed police officers literally filled our church to overflowing, lining the room and even listening by loudspeakers in the parking lot.

As the service was beginning, I sat in the front row not just extremely nervous but exceedingly intimidated. Then as I walked to the stage, something suddenly happened.

My overwhelming self-consciousness was instantly replaced with overwhelming calm. I knew I was on assignment and compelled to speak. The words I had carefully prepared were no longer merely mine but words empowered from on high. There was a much deeper, stronger voice at work. I knew it, as did everyone else. I'm told that many officers came to faith that day and that those in the room have never forgotten the impact of that moment.

You don't have to be in ministry to struggle with fear, anxiety, and uncertainty. These are universal emotions regardless of your profession or calling.

The good news is that fear, anxiety, and uncertainty are not leadership *dis*qualifiers; rather, in many ways they are actually leadership *qualifiers*. In other words, they qualify us once we realize that something is more important than whatever we fear: our reverence for the high calling of God. As the apostle Paul said, "When I am weak, then I am strong."

If God wants you to have greater influence, He will probably allow you to face greater challenges. I once shared a message in which I told of a five-month series of crises I endured early in my ministry. It seemed like everything erupted in the church at once: the death of a baby, the molestation of an adolescent by a trusted family friend and church leader, the murder of a key volunteer, and the discovery of immorality deep within the leadership core.

Years later, after I briefly referenced this litany of tragedies from long ago in another church, a business leader immediately came to me. Mike said, "Unless a leader has been tested, I can't really trust him. Now I know that I can trust you."

Everything that we *go through* we are to *grow through*. Everything that happens to us is not just *for now* but *for later*.

It's not just *for us* but *for others*. So, have you ever been embarrassed by a failure or, worse, been ashamed of yourself? After the apostle Peter denied the Lord three times, Peter no doubt cratered in shame, wondering how he could ever be of value to the Lord again. However, on the back side of a soul-crushing failure, God used Peter far beyond anything prior. He had to be greatly broken before becoming a greater blessing.

The same was true for Saul of Tarsus who became Paul the apostle. After his stunning conviction and conversion, he was chosen for the special assignment of sharing the gospel with the Gentiles. It was then the Lord said, "And I will show him how much he must suffer for my name's sake" (Acts 9:16).

Being of greater service is usually preceded by experiencing greater suffering. I can relate to that, and you probably can too. None of us will ever be stressless, flawless, or pain free. Hard stuff happens to everyone. Testing times come to all.

Many people are being tested at a whole new level due to the pandemic, and the testing is not without value. James said, "Consider it pure joy, my brothers and sisters, whenever you face trials of many kinds, because you know that the testing of your faith produces perseverance. Let perseverance finish its work so that you may be mature and complete, not lacking anything" (James 1:2–4 NIV).

Tested leaders are the only ones truly qualified to lead anything. When our church faced a severe financial crisis, some wondered whether our ministry would even survive.

Even though we were solidly in the megachurch category at
the time, we were engulfed in a mega-million-dollar difficulty.
We had just opened a $20 million extension campus. At the
same time, we were immersed in a multimillion-dollar land use
battle with Boulder County that went all the way to the steps of
the U.S. Supreme Court.

All this happened in 2008 just as the economy cratered.
We were forced to lay off 40 percent of our staff immediately
and then another 25 percent the year after.

The church was reeling, and so was I. That's when I was
seized by the words of 2 Peter 1:3 (NIV) and had them bold-
ly stenciled on my office wall: "His divine power has given us
everything we need for life and godliness."

I looked at that verse multiple times a day and often clung
to it throughout the day. In fact, I often affirmed the implica-
tions of it out loud to my assistant . . . and especially to myself!

- "We've got all the *money* today to do everything
  God wants us to do . . . today!"
- "We've got all the *resources* today to do everything
  God wants us to do . . . today!"
- "We've got all the *time* today to do everything
  God wants us to do . . . today!"

Dallas Willard has said, "In my experience the illuminating
word given to me by God is often spoken by me." Sometimes
we hear ourselves say surprising things. That happens often

in safe settings when we feel accepted. In covenant groups it's not uncommon for someone to admit, "I've never told anyone this before."

God's Word *to* us is often God's Word spoken *through* us! These aren't merely encouraging words that we seize; rather, they are God's words that seize us. Every time I saw God's promise printed on my wall, it seemed to come right off the wall and into my reality. I didn't just remember that it was in the Bible; I experienced it in my heart.

There's a difference between the Greek word *gnosis,* meaning "knowledge," and *epignosis,* meaning "experiential knowledge." One refers to intellectually comprehending truth. The other, to full knowledge, discernment, and recognition of ultimate reality in one's heart. It's a higher degree of intensity, a deep energy of understanding. It's knowing that you know something to the center of your being.

What do you know to the center of you? It seems that the things we know at the deepest level, those things that penetrate our hearts, are the things we haven't merely casually observed but rather learned in the deep cauldron of life's pain. These truths, learned through intense suffering and difficulty, have shaped us—and when shared by us most help to shape the hearts of others.

As Oswald Chambers has observed in his book *My Utmost for His Highest,* "If you're going to be used by God, he will take you through a number of experiences that are not meant for you personally at all. They are designed to make you useful in his hands, and to enable you to understand what takes place in the lives of others. …God's way is always the way of suffering—the way of the long road home."

PAIN GIVES US A PLATFORM

Those who are struggling right now need to pursue the higher calling that is often to be found in and after the suffering. As Oswald Chambers said, "Then comes the surprise—'Why, He was there all the time, and I never knew it!' Never live for the rare moments, they are surprises."[3]

Recently I met with one of the officers called to the scene of the mass shooting where ten died at a grocery store in Boulder, Colorado. Brad was one of the first to arrive on the scene as shots were being fired and glass was raining down. In the middle of the ugly, he helped drag the fallen officer out of the firefight.

Brad was one of the heroes on the front lines that day. In fact, he was the one who took the shooter into custody and accompanied him in the ambulance to the hospital. It's a moment he will never forget and one he will forever relive.

My encouragement and challenge to Brad was to leverage what he's learned for the good of other officers in the future. That's the ultimate credential of nobility, enduring the worst and yet serving still.

God doesn't waste our pain when we are willing to do something with it, to learn from it and then move forward to help others in similar situations. As we've heard it said, "If we're not dead, we're not done. As long as we have a pulse, we have a purpose." Those of us who have endured anything from personal attacks to panic attacks, physical battles to legal battles, emotional heartaches to physical heart attacks know that our stories can help bring benefit to others. As Paul said, He "comforts us in all our troubles so that we can comfort others" (2 Corinthians 1:4 NIV).

OUR STORIES OF PAIN AND STRUGGLE CONNECT US

Certainly, our stories of struggle connect us. When we simply share our successes, we are in danger of becoming competitors. When we share our struggles, we become true friends.

Our vulnerable stories connect us at a heart level. Unless and until we open up our hearts to others in safe community, we cannot find true healing from God.

It's in safe community where we discover that we're heart connected. We're not the only one who feels confused, angry, inadequate, or afraid. We must learn to articulate our pain so that we can also articulate our learning. This in turn helps to bring healing both for ourselves and for others.

In his book *The Wounded Healer*, Henri Nouwen says the key word is *articulation*.

This articulation, I believe, is the basis for a spiritual leadership of the future, because only he who is able to articulate his own experience can offer himself to others as a source of clarification. The Christian leader is, therefore, a man who is willing to put his own articulated faith at the disposal of those who ask his help. In this sense he is a servant of servants, because he is the first to enter the promised but dangerous land, the first to tell those who are afraid what he has seen, heard and touched. . . . The great illusion of leadership is to think that man can be led out of the desert by someone who has never been there.[4]

At best we are all "wounded healers"!

Don't underestimate the power of your personal story. Each of us has a story that highlights the amazing grace of God. Your story doesn't have to be dramatic, but it must true. I've heard soul-shaping stories from leaders that span the emotional spectrum. Everything from enduring house fires to helicopter crashes, personal immorality to imprisonment, pornography addiction to devastating affairs.

What these stories all hold in common is that their life-altering pain was neither fatal nor final. Those who have humbly shared them are each rebounding now to greater levels of effectiveness. While they deeply lament their stumbles and failures, they rejoice in how God has leveraged their learnings both for themselves and for others. They've done the hard work of heart work, and therefore, they are equipped to serve as physicians of the soul. As one leader said, "I regret the things I did for what they were but not for what they did in me."

Dr. Matthew LaGrange is definitely in that category. When we first meaningfully connected, I thought he was merely curious about the concept of covenant groups. He shocked me when he said, "No, I get what they are, I want to know how I can get in one!"

As a psychologist, Matthew leads a burgeoning ministry of over two dozen counselors called His Story Coaching and Counseling. He often shares his own personal story of struggle when speaking with other leaders, but seldom at the depth he did in the covenant group of mine that he joined. The more he shared, the more the group coalesced.

Our stories not only connect us but can even catapult us to greater impact and influence for Christ. It's not because we may have done everything perfectly or even confidently. Far from it. It's only when we realize we haven't always done the best we knew to do, and humbly acknowledge our failures and flaws, that God's grace and mercy flow.

As King Solomon wisely reminds us, "Whoever conceals their sins does not prosper, but the one who confesses and renounces them finds mercy" (Proverbs 28:13 NIV).

Make no mistake: when you own it, your pain can become your platform! The very thing that haunts you, or inhibits you, or leaves you feeling lesser than others may actually be a gift for enabling deeper connections with others.

BUT ARE WE "GOOD ENOUGH"?

When I was younger, I often struggled with the question of being good enough. As a skinny, insecure kid growing up in Chicago, I never felt like I quite measured up. I was never good enough to make the high school team, impress all the cute girls, or earn straight As. Sadly, even now that I'm much older, I sometimes still struggle with this. Maybe you can relate.

What's worse, I never felt like I measured up in the eyes of God. When I was baptized at the age of eight, I wanted forgiveness for not being good enough and to avoid the penalty of hell. Many people today don't seem to have that concern. In many ways we live in a grace-saturated culture. These days few people, young or old, seem to struggle much with the salvation issue. Perhaps it's just assumed that everyone deserves an eternal trophy just for showing up at death's door.

Now it seems the issue of "good enough" has a new twist. Here's how Anthony Bradley, professor at The King's College, put it when describing the attitude of our time among young Christians:

It's not necessarily, "Am I good enough to escape eternal punishment?" It's rather, "Am I good enough to fulfill the mission that I've been told constitutes being a good Christian or a great Christian?" So, 'Am I a good Christian if I'm not a senator, a judge, saving orphans from sex slavery in India? If I'm not doing something extraordinary for God, then I'm not good enough. So my life has to be Snap-chat or Instagram-worthy to be impressive and sufficient for the Lord."[5]

Few seem to be content with their level of influence. That's not only true for young college students but also for seasoned leaders. Not one of the many pastors I know thinks his church is large enough, social media platform popular enough, or influence broad enough. We live in a world of constant comparison, and we often feel like we just don't measure up.

This is a debilitating and worldwide problem. I was intrigued by an article in *World* magazine on the topic of Japanese "Shut-ins." It wasn't about old folks in their declining years confined to home. It was about young men who failed to succeed in the highly competitive Japanese business culture.

These young men have become hermits. They are hiding at home in shame with no jobs, no friends, and no hopes for their future. Sadly, their parents are also embarrassed by their sons' failure to excel, and they try to keep it a secret from the world. Christian missionaries are now seeking to reach these forgotten young men with the gospel—the message of acceptance that is not based on performance.[6]

Clearly, it's not our performance for Christ that ultimately matters but our position in Christ. Those of us with a bent toward self-condemnation need to be reminded daily that there is no condemnation for those in Christ. And as we read in 1 John 3:20 (NIV), "If our hearts condemn us, . . . God is greater than our hearts."

For years I misunderstood this. I assumed that since He knows it all, each and every flaw, I'm really in trouble! Now I see that verse 20 is preceded by verse 19, which says, "we set our hearts at rest in his presence" (1 John 3:19–20 NIV). Let's face it, there is *only* rest for us in God's gracious acceptance of our daily failures.

We all need to hear this message because we all have our limitations. No one is always going to be in first place in every category. That's why we all need to hear, ponder, and apply the gospel daily. Our standing before God is not a matter of résumé but relationship.

DON'T DESPISE THE SMALL THINGS

If I am important to God only if I'm doing or leading something really big, then I'm in really big trouble!

Today I no longer lead an impressive and growing ministry reaching thousands. I now work behind the scenes as a sort of undercover pastor. That means I'm no longer in the lead role. Now I'm in a support role. I'm learning to embrace obscurity and find my fulfillment in personal relationships, not in organizational leadership.

One former megachurch pastor is now redefining success. Greg thought that at age fifty-five he would be in a much different place with much more visibility and influence. He not only assumed it, he desired it.

His life has taken a different turn. Now he finds himself serving in a far smaller setting. Ironically, he is surprisingly more fulfilled. He is discovering the joy of discipling as Jesus did.

Jesus led a small group. Shockingly, He never served as lead pastor of a megachurch. Jesus chose to go deeper with fewer.

Here's the template of transformation:

- Go small.
- Go slow.
- Go strong.

This is not a slam against megachurches or those who lead them. I once led one, and you may belong to one. The point is that if Jesus were to have started His redemptive mission now, in the twenty-first century rather than the first century, how might He do that?

Would He arrange to fill the twelve largest venues in the world? Or might he choose to fill twelve followers with the gospel? Twelve who would then do the same with others? We know the answer.

Not long ago another pastor was gripped with the clarity of "go small, go slow, and go strong," and it changed everything! The simplicity of this pattern motivated him and his entire leadership team to reconsider how they would each lead and serve in their large church.

Think about when and where you have had the most heart-touching experiences. Almost without exception the most formational experiences probably occurred in the smallest of settings. Our families, our friends, our trusted circles of confidants have shaped us all the most. That's where we feel loved, not for what we do but for who we are.

Everyone is valuable to God regardless of performance and status, even pastors, even you! The gospel compels us to strive, serve, and even succeed—not in order to impress God and others but rather because we are loved by God and have already been declared to be of immense value to Him.

Here's the shockingly good news: Our value is based not on our achievement but on His acceptance. Jesus made that clear when He said, "You are more valuable to God than a whole flock of sparrows" (Matthew 10:31). Since God takes note of little sparrows and values them, then there is hope for us all!

Repeat this out loud: "God takes note of even me and values even me!"

I'm now accepting that only by the atoning death of Christ and God's declaration that I am His beloved child will I ever have confidence that I am finally good enough. In short, without grace there is no peace. That's God's Story and it's now my story, and I'm staking my life and eternity on it!

REFLECTION QUESTIONS

Have you ever struggled with feeling "good enough to belong"?
What happened?

When have you felt most inadequate?

Has your definition of success ever changed? Describe what happened.

CHAPTER 2

LIVE HEART-STRONG

"THE BEST AND MOST BEAUTIFUL THINGS IN THE
WORLD CANNOT BE SEEN OR EVEN TOUCHED—
THEY MUST BE FELT WITH THE HEART."

—HELEN KELLER

W ho knows you well enough to know the true condition of your heart and soul? We're not just talking about the things that matter most to you but about the inner you—who you are at the core. Heart and soul are frequently linked in the Scriptures. In the book *Unhindered: Aligning the Story of Your Heart*, by my friends Drs. Charity Byers and John Walker, we're reminded of that: "We can learn a lot from Scripture about the heart. The word *heart* is used 570 times in the NIV Bible, and it is most often used metaphorically to describe the inner self, just as we're defining it, the place where feelings, thinking, longings and willpower meet.

The biblical writers often refer to the heart as the place of our personhood, our true selves."[7]

I used to think that heart language was about *weaker* things; now I know it's about *stronger* things. It's really about the dominating desires of your life. It's not about sentimentality but about energy and vitality.

Through her research and books, Brené Brown helped me to understand that heart language is strongly connected to courage. She calls attention to the fact that at its core courage is really about speaking all of one's mind by sharing all of one's heart. Needless to say, those sorts of conversations are both risky and rare.

Heart health is not accidental; it is intentional. King David wrote in Psalm 138:3 (NIV 1984 Edition), "When I called, you answered me; you made me bold and stouthearted." Fundamentally it is God who is the essential source of our heart health and strength. But how does God actually increase our heart health and strength? He does that through the only two things that are eternal: His Word and His people!

No one can ever be heart healthy alone. We all need others to sharpen, encourage, resource, and connect us. At times we even need others to challenge us to listen to our hearts so that we can lead from our hearts.

"LISTEN TO YOUR HEART!"

Just as many people resist scheduling an annual physical exam, most people are also reluctant to submit to anything resembling a spiritual exam. If feedback is the breakfast of champions, they prefer to skip breakfast as they rush into their day. Maybe it's because they don't want to receive an honest assessment, or maybe it's because they don't know who to ask.

After speaking for a national conference once, I asked a resident scholar for his feedback on my messages. I asked him, "If God might be trying to get a message to me, through you, what might it be?" I was stunned by his candid insight: "Yes, I do have something . . . in the Bible heart and mind are frequently linked, but heart almost always comes first. You have a good, fleshy heart. Listen to your heart!"

Who talks like that? Well, if he had been some sort of New Age guru I encountered on the street in Boulder, Colorado, I would have easily dismissed him. But he wasn't rooted in the occult; rather, he was steeped in the study of the Scriptures in the original Greek! In addition, he had just listened to me preach, teach, and converse over the course of several hours. He had the credentials to get my attention, and in that moment, I knew what his message meant. I was grappling with some serious challenges at the time that he knew nothing about, yet his observation gave me the courage to live righteously and stay the course regarding those challenges, no matter what.

SHARE MORE OF YOUR HEART

When facing giant challenges, do you tend to live and lead more with your head or with your heart? In a recent coaching call, a good friend talked about his current drains connecting with the elders and staff on his leadership team. The more he shared, the more concerned I became. Oddly, by the end of the call, I was more agitated than he was—and we were talking about his problems, not mine!

That's when I asked him, "Are you more of a head leader or a heart leader?" He paused and admitted that in the face of troubling trends and leadership issues, he tended to take more of a "head up" approach. That is, he rarely lost sleep over things because he just didn't let much bother him. Well, that led me to want to "bother" him myself! I challenged him to share more of his heart with those in his leadership circle.

Do those closest to you know your heart? Do they know when you're dealing with deep disappointment? Do they know when you're feeling frustrated or hurt, overwhelmed or under supported? Do they know when you are feeling an inner compulsion or conviction, an unshakable passion or a sense of divine determination?

Those closest to us shouldn't have to guess about our feelings, especially in the face of daunting challenges. Candidly sharing our feelings doesn't mean erupting with anger, but at times it does require openly sharing our concerns and heartfelt convictions with passion.

It's not excusing a lack of discretion; it's about the need for transparent congruence. There should always be a linkage between our head and our heart. We're called to have both the mind of Christ and also a heart of courage. Sometimes silence isn't golden, it's ungodly! Every godly leader knows that some situations require boldness.

ARE YOU HEART-STRONG OR HEAD-STRONG?

When I recently pondered the story of David and Goliath, I realized that David had boldness while Goliath had bravado. No one was willing to face the nine-foot-nine enemy of the living God in battle, not even King Saul, and Saul was the biggest man in Israel both in rank and stature. It wasn't until young David showed up that anyone was willing and able to speak up with the passion and confidence necessary to convince the king to allow him to represent the entire nation in one-on-one combat. You know how the story goes. As someone once said, while everyone else saw a giant too big to face, David saw a target too big to miss!

Sometimes it may seem presumptuous to face a giant of any sort until you see the greater purpose. What I've learned is that when facing a challenge far beyond myself, the key is trusting the One who is far bigger still!

David challenged Goliath not just with his sling and a small stone but in the mighty name of the living God. David wasn't just *head*-strong; David was *heart*-strong. This is why God said, "I have found David son of Jesse, a man after my own heart" (Acts 13:22 NIV).

Are you more head-strong or heart-strong? It's an important question. In another coaching call recently, I was asked to define the difference between head-strong and heart-strong. After fumbling around a moment, I suggested a head-strong leader approaches challenges with a cocky attitude of "I've got this!" By contrast, the heart-strong leader lives and leads with the humble conviction, "God's got this!"

Bravado is *head up*; boldness is *heart up*. Bravado is haughty; boldness is humble. Goliath had bravado; David had boldness. David was incensed that a pagan bully was intimidating the people of God. David's response was not to join the majority who were cowering in fear but to stand up with the conviction that God would bring victory. Why? David knew that the victory would not be accomplished *by* him but rather by God *through* him. David was heart-strong!

ASK GOD FOR A HOLY BOLDNESS

While I'm definitely not a warrior leader like David, I have had many experiences similar to David's. Despite my leadership insecurities and my lingering feelings of inadequacy, on multiple occasions something extraordinary has happened in and through me. I know that I could never have said what I said, done what I did, or overcome what I overcame unless God was at work in and through me.

I know what it is to be consumed with a sort of holy boldness. What's notable to me is that on those occasions I didn't try to convince myself to be bold; rather, God surprised me by making me bold. That's how I knew it wasn't me but Him!

Why should it surprise any of us when we're told that the same power that raised Jesus from the dead is at work in those who follow Jesus? The fact of the resurrection isn't just a past-tense experience; it is present tense. Easter forever changes everything! Even though we accept the reality of giant problems and recognize our own weakness to fix them, we also know that our God is bigger than any nine-foot-nine giant we will ever face.

Leaders, take heart: everything isn't up to you. God is at work! The apostle Paul reminds us that the same power that raised Jesus from the dead is at work in those who believe! When you become convinced of that, you won't have much trouble convincing anyone else. The challenge for many is not so much mastering material for a message but being mastered by it!

Are you living the life you are calling others to live? We're reminded in James 3:1, "Not many of you should become teachers in the church, for we who teach will be judged more strictly." While God's moral standards are the same for all, the standard for teachers is higher when it comes to practicing what we preach to others. The greatest lecture is the one you live, not merely the one you give. God's people should actually expect us to eat our own cooking and faithfully apply our own preaching to our own lives. This is what makes it so tough to preach with moral authority on any topic such as money or marriage, compassion or contentment, prayer or purity. Every time we grapple with a theme in preparation for a lesson or a message, we go through a personal heart challenge. We have to ask ourselves, *Do I really believe this, and if so, what am I doing about it?*

HEART WORK IS HARD WORK—BUT SO WORTH IT!

Heart work is hard work. No one should ever agree to lead anything unless they are willing to wrestle with matters of the heart. John Flavel once wrote, "The greatest difficulty in conversion is winning the heart to God and after to keep the heart with God. Heart work is hard work indeed."

Those acquainted with heart work know just how demanding it is. It demands the core of you, not just some of you. Often, after a few hours of intense conversation at our soul care retreats, some need to take a nap. That's not just because they're coming out of high stress to the high altitude of Colorado but because of the high demand to process heavy things. Soul care isn't for sissies.

It's why each time we gather as a covenant group, we begin most every session by checking in with a descriptive word or phrase followed with a personal declaration, "I'm all in!" Here's just a sample of the sorts of things I and others have said:

- I'm hopeful . . . and I'm all in!
- I'm exhausted . . . but I'm all in!
- I'm gratified . . . and I'm all in!
- I'm defeated . . . but I'm all in!
- I'm exploring . . . and I'm all in!
- I'm frustrated . . . but I'm all in!

- I'm ready . . . and I'm all in!
- I'm confused . . . but I'm all in!
- I'm anticipating . . . and I'm all in!
- I'm distracted . . . but I'm trying to be all in!
- I'm thriving . . . and I'm all in!

Heart work involves bringing all of who you are with you into a conversation. I often finish a deep connection by saying, "If this were the last conversation we ever had, is there anything else you need to hear from me or you need to say to me?" That's not something that happens quickly in a crowded coffee shop.

Wholehearted conversation requires a safe place and an unhurried pace. Frankly, that's sacred ground, and that ground must be cultivated. Relationships like this are by definition rare ones because they demand the best of us all. They demand our hearts.

How long has it been since you experienced a wholehearted connection with a trusted ally? As a leader this isn't just nice, it is necessary. It isn't just optional, it's essential. It isn't just to happen occasionally, it should happen frequently. This is the essence of your calling. After all, as Jonathan Edwards wrote, "The first and greatest work of a Christian is about his heart."

HEART TRIUMPHS SKILL

How healthy is your heart right now? It doesn't matter whether we lead in a church-related ministry, a business enterprise, or even our own family; sad stuff happens. What matters most is our heart condition. While most leadership books focus on topics related to strategy and skill, the most important and enlightening Book of all puts the emphasis first on heart and soul: "And David shepherded them with integrity of heart; with skillful hands he led them" (Psalm 78:72 NIV).

The sequence is important. It's not coincidental that *heart* comes before skill. In my mentoring and coaching of leaders far and wide, I've learned that what most of them crave is not mere leadership tips but soul-enriching, heart-challenging conversations. We all need these to process the hits and hurts of life and leadership.

What we all know is that families, ministries, and businesses crater not primarily because of strategy mistakes but because of self-centeredness and sin. "The heart is deceitful above all things and beyond cure. Who can understand it?" (Jeremiah 17:9 NIV).

We see this confirmed every day with the news of national leaders crashing due to moral failure. It happens among the media elite, the top CEOs of business, and sadly, even in the senior leadership of the church. The Me Too movement set off shock waves not just among secular leaders but among religious ones as well. *World Magazine* reported on the tragedy and trauma. Its September 15, 2018, cover claimed, "As Pope Francis comes under fire, Protestants in the U.S. face a church-too movement."

The church I loved and led for twenty-nine years was not exempt. We had our own embarrassments and even shame due to the moral failure of several key leaders over the years. A youth intern was even sentenced to prison for molesting minors. These were gut-wrenching and heartbreaking experiences for many, especially for the individuals and families directly involved.

Sadly, it wasn't just the reputation of those who sinned that took a hit; the entire church suffered. The members within the body of Christ are inter-related. When one of us determines to live selfishly or sin grievously, all of us suffer some of the collateral damage.

THE LINK BETWEEN HEART HEALTH AND TRANSPARENCY

Can you honestly say, "I have no secrets, and it is well with my soul"? I often ask this penetrating question from author Jerry Bridges when I'm with my closest colleagues. Only those who know us best would ever dare ask that question of us.

- Who might *ask you* that question?
- Who might *you ask* that question?

Soul care isn't brain surgery; it's harder . . . because it's a matter of the heart. Sadly, some Christian leaders have big heads and small hearts. "Shop talk" can be a good thing, but it can also be just a "heady" thing. By contrast, soul care is more of a heart thing, especially focusing on insight, illumination, and transformation.

With these truths about soul care in mind, there are three essential ingredients in the recipe for transformational covenant groups:

- Courageous candor must be led. Once again, As Henri Nouwen shares in *The Wounded Healer*, "Only he who is able to articulate his own experience can offer himself to others as a source of clarification. The Christian leader is, therefore, first of all, a man who is willing to put his own articulated faith at the disposal of those who ask for his help. In this sense he is a servant of servants, because he is the first to enter the promised but dangerous land, the first to tell those who are afraid what he has seen, heard and touched."[8]

- Humble vulnerability must be modeled. In his masterpiece entitled *Ruthless Trust*, Brennan Manning makes it clear: "The way of trust is a movement into obscurity, into the undefined, into ambiguity, not into some pre-determined clearly delineated plan for the future . . . the reality of naked trust is the life of the pilgrim who leaves what is nailed down, obvious, and secure, and walks into the unknown without any rational explanation to justify the decision or guarantee the future. Why? Because God has signaled the movement and offered it His presence and His promise."[9]

• Deep, nonjudgmental listening is essential to building trust. Just before every group member shares his in-depth update during every soul care retreat, we repeatedly quote the words of Dr. Karl Menninger to one another, "Listening is a magnetic and strange thing, a creative force. The friends who listen to us are the ones we move toward. When [we feel] we are listened to, it creates us, makes us unfold and expand."

Leaders crave community but rarely experience it. That's because achieving this kind of intimacy of soul within a group doesn't happen easily or automatically. It must be intentionally led, sincerely embraced, and fiercely guarded.

YOUR HEART IS INTUITIVE

Heart talk isn't mushy, it's intuitive. "Who gives intuition to the heart and instinct to the mind?" (Job 38:36). Researchers have discovered that there are more neural pathways moving from the heart to the head than from the head to the heart. Some talk about the brain as if in the heart: "The heart has its own independent nervous system, referred to as 'the brain in the heart.' There are forty thousand neurons in the heart—as many as found in various subcortical centers in the brain."[10]

That's why we often sense things before we can rationally explain them.

The words of Blaise Pascal have long been quoted: "The heart has its reasons which reason knows nothing of. We know the truth not only by the reason, but by the heart." That is, we sometimes quickly intuit things emotionally before we can carefully reason them through intellectually. Interestingly, the word *emotion* literally means "energy in motion."

In the book *The HeartMath Solution,* the authors point out that the feeling world moves at a higher speed than the mind: "For centuries, poets and philosophers have sensed that the heart is at the center of our lives. Saint-Exupery wrote, 'And now here is my secret, a very simple secret; it is only with the heart that one can see rightly; what is essential is invisible to the eye.'"[11]

Clearly, there is more to intelligence and vision than merely brain power and physical sight. We may feel or sense fear before we actually see the reason. That's how many bad accidents are avoided—and bad decisions as well. That's why we need to listen to the wisdom of others.

A couple Linda and I knew well were paying a high price for not listening well. Even though he was an experienced and savvy investor, on two occasions his wife was unsettled about a financial decision he insisted on making. Against her strong advice, her husband made two major financial investments, both of which she opposed and both of which led to major financial losses. Even though he had more of a brain for business, she had more sensitivity of heart.

Believers should all learn to listen better to the prompts of the Spirit because Christ is at work in us. The apostle Paul reminds us 216 times in his books that we are in Christ or that Christ is in us, and the gospel writer John reminds us another sixteen times. There are only two categories of people: those in Adam and those in Christ. If Christ is your Lord, that not only cements your identify but it clarifies your reality.

The key is Christ in us. There is a mystical union between every believer and Christ: the two are intertwined. "But whoever is united with the Lord is one with him in spirit" (1 Corinthians 6:17 NIV). Living with a strong, intuitive heart means tuning in to the Spirit within us.

HEART, SOUL, MIND, AND STRENGTH

While heart, mind, soul, and strength are at times used interchangeably, or perhaps in a string in the same breath, they are each distinct. Combined together, they compose the entirety of our being.

Mark 12:30 (ESV) presents it like this: "And you shall love the Lord your God with all your heart and with all your soul and with all your mind and with all your strength."

I find it helpful to picture this as a Venn diagram composed of four intersecting circles with Christ's Spirit in the center:

- Heart = our innermost being. The essence of a person includes his or her feelings and deepest passions.
- Soul = the entire person. You don't merely have a soul; you are a soul. It connects with everything.
- Mind = the mental capacity. The mind has ability to reason, analyze, and understand truth.
- Strength = the body. Our body has the physical capacity to engage actively as servants of God in a physical world.

In his book *Soul Keeping*, John Ortberg tells of a conversation with his mentor Dallas Willard. Dallas said, "The soul is the capacity to integrate all the parts into a single, whole life. It is something like a program that runs a computer, you don't usually notice it unless it messes up."

He added, "The soul is that aspect of your whole being that correlates, iintegrates, and enlivens everything going on in the various dimensions of the self. The soul life is the life center of human beings." [12]

He illustrated with concentric circles:

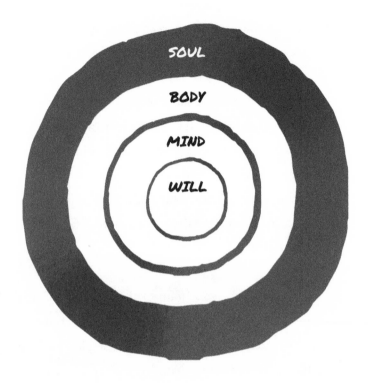

Will (the inner circle)

Mind (the second circle)

Body (the third circle)

Soul (the fourth or outer all-encompassing circle)

John Ortberg summarizes the soul like this: "A soul is healthy—well ordered—when there is harmony between these three entities and God's intent for all creation. When you are connected with God and other people in life, you have a healthy soul."[13]

How would you rate the health of your soul?

That's the question I recently asked six men as they wrapped up a three-year journey together in a soul-enriching covenant group. On a scale of one to ten, they each assessed themselves at a level eight. This health improvement happened during the COVID-19 crisis! Amazingly, the two who said their soul health escalated the most were the two oldest members of the group!

Soul health matters at any age, and the number of our days are not guaranteed.

My friend died of a heart attack at age fifty-one. John Seitz was in my first ever covenant group where we talked often about heart health. He and his wife knew he had heart issues, but they were confident the good doctors at Mayo Clinic would take good care of him. But the same week he was scheduled to return for a checkup, and possible surgery, he suddenly died.

John's funeral was amazing, and few have ever hit me as hard. He referred to me as his spiritual father, which makes him my spiritual son. I knew him exceedingly well and therefore could say with confidence that John finished well, more in love with Jesus at the end than at the beginning.

Who knows you well enough to confidently assess the condition of your soul, the essence and the core of the real you? It's what's at the center of you that matters the most, "which is Christ in you the hope of glory" (Colossians 1:27 NIV). Ultimately, Christ is to be the all-consuming center of our lives. Nothing matters more for now and eternity than Him. One day soon that will be stunningly clear to us all.

REFLECTION QUESTIONS

Are you more of a head leader or a heart leader? What does that look like in your daily life?

Would you describe yourself as highly intuitive? Why or why not?

How would you assess the health of your soul?

CHAPTER 3

CHOOSE YOUR CIRCLES

"NOT WITHSTANDING ALL THE PRAISE
I WAS RECEIVING WHILE SPEAKING ABOUT
COMMUNITY, I DIDN'T FEEL THAT I TRULY
BELONGED TO ANYONE."

—HENRI NOUWEN

---

ere's a revolutionary thought: Your true "belongings" are not your possessions, but your relationships, the people to whom you belong and who belong to you.[14] That's a summary of the insights coming from a book I enjoyed a few years ago entitled *The Search to Belong* in which Joseph Myers shares a study done back in the 1960s by Edward T. Hall about the four spheres of belonging.

Several times recently I've introduced this concept to leaders and watched the lights come on. Picture the four spheres of belonging as four concentric rings of a circle:

SPHERES OF BELONGING

PUBLIC SPHERE
12 FEET AND BEYOND

SOCIAL SPHERE
4 TO 12 FEET

PERSONAL SPHERE
18 INCHES TO 4 FEET

INTIMATE SPHERE
0 TO 18 INCHES

- The Public Space is the outer ring. That could be our neighborhood, the coffee shop, lobby of a large church. It's a place where we frequently find ourselves mingling, a place where we recognize familiar faces. That's the public sphere.

- The Social Space is the next ring inward. This might be a Sunday school class or a small group that gathers in a home. It's not necessarily an intense gathering; it's a friendly one filled with people with whom we interact. It's where relaxed laughter comes easily. That's the social sphere.

- The Personal Space is the ring near the center. This is the table at a coffee shop or restaurant with a free flow of information and updates that might go beyond general things to some private things. That's the personal sphere.
- The Intimate Space is at the center. This is where the most in-depth stuff occurs and where the naked truth is shared. This is the rarest of all and the most vulnerable of all.

It's in our intimate space that the most significant transformation occurs. It's not just a safe space for the sharing of our most painful experiences. It's a safe space for deep reflection about those experiences and the articulation that leads to illumination. This is sacred space.

WHO IS AT YOUR TABLE?

We are not alone—in fact, if we would just open our eyes to see, most of us would say that we are relationally blessed and amazingly well resourced. One of my mentors, Bob Shank, opened my eyes to this reality when he introduced me to the idea of "a table of influence." Those with seats at this table don't have to be in the same location or even know one another. The key is not their relationship with each other but to you.

We all need to sit in a circle of trust with those who love us and respect us but aren't always impressed by us! C.S. Lewis said, "The next best thing to being wise oneself is to live in a circle of those who are."

Who sits in the circle at your table? All of us have those who enjoy positions of highest influence in our lives. They may not all have been invited to your table; some may have invited themselves. They may not all be healthy, noble, or insightful, but the ones we most value certainly are.

The company we keep influences us the most. It's called the "sociology of desire." That is, we tend to gravitate toward the tastes, preferences, values, and attitudes of those we hang around with and listen to the most. Check it out and you'll probably see how this is true for you. We all take clues from those around us, and often without even realizing it, we adapt and assimilate what we see in them or hear from them.

- Those with a strong work ethic inspire us to work both harder and smarter.
- Those with depth of insight and uncommon wisdom inspire us to study and reflect more.
- Those with exceptional generosity prompt us to excel in the grace of giving.
- Those who have happy and healthy relationships cause us to imitate their commitment to investing in life-giving friendships.

One of the positive dimensions of our technological connectivity is the access we all have to life-giving people. They might not work with you or live next door to you, but they are certainly available to you. They're just one email, phone call, or Zoom connect away. You are the one in charge of your relational calendar. Who are you seeking to grow deeper along with you? Here's a crazy thought: instead of waiting on others to reach out to you, reach out to others!

CHOOSING QUALITY OVER QUANTITY

How many quality relationships do you enjoy? Sadly, we live in an age of amazing technological connection yet soul-depleting personal disconnection. While many have hundreds of Facebook friends, most have few face-to-face, personal friends. Many lament that they have no close friends at all, and the same is true even among Christian leaders. We're facing what some call an epidemic of loneliness!

One leader just admitted to me that he sometimes struggles with "friend envy." That's because his wife has several deep friendships with other women, and he has none with other men.

Heart-to-heart friendships are rare among men, especially among those in leadership positions. Pastors are certainly among those who talk the most about community and quality connections but enjoy it the least. We often talk about what we long for—we crave community because we were made for it—it's the hunger of our heart. We all seek to be known, understood, and meaningfully connected.

However, when you ponder this concept, you may even come to see that you are more relationally blessed than you had realized. When you consider how God has blessed you through the years and even in recent days, see who comes to mind. Who is sitting at your table of influence right now or has in the recent past? After first learning this from Bob Shank's The Master's Program, here's how I have adapted and expanded my mentor's model (by the way, people can shift seats from time to time, or even occupy more than one of these four important seats):

- The Work Chair: Those who sharpen you. These are the ones who inspire you to improve both in your efficiency and your effectiveness. "As iron sharpens iron, so one person sharpens another" (Proverbs 27:17 NIV). Who sharpens you?

- The Wisdom Chair: Those who deepen you. These are the ones who take you deeper by asking you uncommon questions and by modeling uncommon candor. They may not always be the smartest people at your table, but they're likely to be among the most curious and honest. Who deepens you?

- The Well-Being Chair: Those who enrich you. These are the ones who have a pattern of happily blessing and uplifting you. They may share their resources but, even more, their hearts, their homes, and even their good humor. Who enriches you?

- The "W.O.O." Chair: W.O.O. is an abbreviation for "winning others over" and refers to those who connect you with others who are good for you and fun for you. Friends love to introduce their friends to the friends who open up opportunities for them. Who connects you?

News flash: your life will never be any richer than your relationships! What we know is that good company is catalytic for good outcomes. In their exceptional devotional based on the book of Proverbs, *God's Wisdom for Navigating Life*, Tim and Kathy Keller share some timely insights on the importance of both intentionality and constancy with regard to friendship. As the Kellers explain, "In the early stage of your life, you were shaped most by your family. But for the rest of your life you will be shaped largely by your friends. You become like the people with whom you spend the most time."[15]

All healthy relationships are for a reason and a season. None will last forever on planet Earth. Seasons and circumstances of life are constantly changing. So, who are your best friends now, the ones who want something *for* you and not just something *from* you?

Who are your sacred allies, your soul-enriching friends? Here are seven clues to help you identify them. Ask yourself these questions:

- *Who breathes life into me rather than sucks life out of me?*
- *Who challenges me spiritually?*
- *Who sharpens me mentally?*
- *Who is a friend of my excitement?*
- *Who makes me laugh?*
- *Who can keep a confidence?*
- *Who leaves me feeling more alive?*

Use the diagram on the following page to help you identify the people who fill these important roles in your life.

My Table of Influence

People who...

...DEEPEN ME

- ....
- ....
- ....

...SHARPEN ME

- ....
- ....
- ....

Wisdom Chair   *Work Chair*

My Confidants

- ....
- ....
- ....

Well-Being Chair   *W.O.O. Chair*

...RESOURCE ME

- ....
- ....
- ....

...CONNECT ME

- ....
- ....
- ....

DEALING WITH TOXIC OR DIFFICULT PEOPLE

Chances are, there are people in your life whose names never occurred to you as you went through that list of questions.

We all know people who are not life-givers to us but life-suckers. They leave us feeling drained, or angry, or sad.

When we are with them, we know we are not the best version of ourselves. And if they bring out the worst in us, we're probably not bringing out the best in them.

Dr. John Walker, the founder of Blessing Ranch Ministries, once said he determined not to invest undue time placating or befriending a toxic person. The reality is that toxic people with toxic attitudes not only abound, they surround us all. That's at least true via our technology if not in our actual community. The key is to minimize those influences by maximizing the life-giving influences of those who bring the best to us and seek the best for us.

I've learned that you will know the difference between a toxic person and a safe one by how you feel after you've been with them. We teach our kids the wisdom of 1 Corinthians 15:33, which says, "Bad company corrupts good character." Researchers call it "emotional contagion." We know that washing up and masking up during a pandemic is a great way to prevent the spread of various airborne infections. What we often fail to recognize is the more serious threats of emotional infection. These can be even more soul depleting.

One way to picture toxic people is with the simple Energy Matrix Chart on the following page. The chart is composed of two categories: activities and relationships. It's clarifying to list for yourself those who are life enriching and therefore above the line, and then those who are consistently life depleting and fall below the line.

THE ENERGY MATRIX

	PEOPLE	ACTIVITIES

ENERGIZING
- ....
- ....
- ....

- ....
- ....
- ....

───────────────────────────────

DEPLETING
- ....
- ....
- ....

- ....
- ....
- ....

While no one can or should always avoid challenging situations and people, it's important that we at least acknowledge them, if only to ourselves. In the May 19 reading of *My Utmost For His Highest*, Oswald Chambers says, "I feel sorry for the Christian who doesn't have something in the circumstances of his life that he wishes were not there."

The calling to us all is not to seek to eliminate every difficult person or circumstance that surrounds us. Rather, we should seek to minimize the soul-stressing impact of these difficult people and circumstances by maximizing the opposite. It's the equivalent of faithfully exercising and enjoying a healthy intake of quality food and even extra vitamins to counteract the depleting effects of normal aging and inevitable illnesses.

So, who are those people for you and what are those activities that fill your soul? We've all got access to various soul-enriching people and activities, but it's up to us to draw benefit from them!

GORDON MACDONALD'S CATEGORIES

I'm indebted to Gordon MacDonald for his concept of people in a church fitting into four distinct categories: very *influential* people, very *teachable* people, very *nice* people, very *draining* people.[16]

I have added one more category: very *rejuvenating* people. There are levels in all of these categories, of course, and once again I've found that the visual of a pyramid, which you'll find on the following page, unlocks my brain as well as the brains of other leaders I've worked with.

PYRAMID OF PEOPLE TYPES

VRP
VERY
REJUVENATING

VIP
VERY INFLUENCIAL

VTP
VERY TEACHABLE

VNP
VERY NICE

VDP
VERY DRAINING
CIRCUMSTANTIALLY DRAINING
CHRONICALLY DRAINING
DIVISIVELY DRAINING

- *Very Rejuvenating People* are the few at the top of the pyramid. These are the top five percent, the ones whom you always want to make time for because they unceasingly rejuvenate you!

- *Very Influential People* are probably in the top 15–20 percent of your organization because they are so influential. Everyone takes their cues from them.

- ***Very Teachable People*** are energizing because they are so receptive. You love talking with them because what you say resonates with them.
- ***Very Nice People*** are the bulk of any organization, and they are just plain nice to have around. They don't lead or stir things up, they simply participate with pleasantness.
- ***Very Draining People*** are the most challenging people. Some would simply be in the category of what I call the *circumstantially draining* people, those who are dealing with unusual health or life issues. The more seriously challenging are what I call the *chronically draining* people who always have a complaint and always want you to know about it. Those at the extreme of this category are what I call the *divisively draining*. Their mission is to sow seeds of discord and division.

At various times we may have all been in each of these categories in our relationships with others. However, for a leader it's imperative that the bulk of emotional energy be invested with those in the top three levels. No leader can ignore any of the categories; however, great caution needs to be exercised with the VDPs at the very bottom. Dr. Henry Cloud deals with this masterfully in his classic book *Necessary Endings*. He devotes an entire chapter to the three types of people, which are described in the book of Proverbs. The chapter is entitled "The Wise, the Foolish and the Evil."

Here's how Dr. Cloud sets this up:

If you are a responsible and loving person, then *you might assume other people are like you—responsible and loving.* They do the right thing, taking responsibility for themselves, for their mistakes, for their work. And they care about other people and how their actions affect those people. That is what you do, right? Right. You have concern about how what you do affects others. So doesn't it make sense that everyone else would be like you and really care? Sure, if you lived on Mars.

But this is planet Earth. And if you are going to succeed in life and business, you have to succeed on this planet, not Mars. The truth is not everyone on planet Earth is like you. Not all take responsibility for themselves or care about how their actions are affecting other people or the mission. Moreover, some are even worse than that. Some people are actually out to do you harm.

Not everyone is in the same category. Dr. Cloud suggests three: the wise, the foolish, and the evil. Perhaps other words come to mind for you. When I began in ministry, it would have been very clarifying if everyone was identified with a label like the ones I shared above. "Hi, I'm rejuvenating!" "I'm influential!" "I'm teachable!" "I'm nice!" "I'm draining!" Even more helpful if some had told me, "Hi, I'm wise. I'm foolish. I'm evil."

The problem is, those clarifiers usually take time to discern. That's why everyone is in desperate need of wisdom in navigating the treacherous relational waters of our time. When I was starting out, there were few seasoned leaders around me to talk with face-to-face. Prior to the advent of the internet, the ones I knew from far away were just that, far away. As I struggled with the various types of people I was called to lead, I was often confused. With few resources available, I often struggled to understand if I was exaggerating the situations surrounding me, and I was puzzled about how to lead well. I yearned to have a seasoned mentor who would help me understand me . . . and then better understand the swirl of relational challenges surrounding me.

MENTORS AND SPIRITUAL PARENTS

We all need help sorting things through. Only when we hear ourselves say certain things out loud do we understand them ourselves. Other times, it's only when we hear someone else candidly share their struggle out loud do we understand them.

That certainly happened for a Swiss psychiatrist named Dr. Paul Tournier. He tells the story in his book *A Place for You*, which was the first book in my soul care journey. It begins with a simple account that gripped me fifty years ago and has never left me:

> The words were those of a young student with whom I formed a deep friendship. He was sitting by my fireside, telling me of his difficulties, of the anxiety that never left him, and which at times turned to panic and to flight. He was trying to look objectively at what was going on inside himself and to understand it. Then, as if summing up his thoughts, he looked up at me and said: "Basically, I'm always looking for a place—for somewhere to be."[17]

I have often longed to sit fireside with a lifelong learner and wise listener who would help me better understand myself. I've been blessed with a variety of soul brothers over the years and have more now than ever. In addition to those in the covenant groups I lead, I also "break bread with the dead" every day. Some of my best mentors are now deceased, but I'm daily enlightened by them. Men like Oswald Chambers, C.S. Lewis, Henri Nouwen, Dallas Willard, and, once again, Dr. Paul Tournier.

I was reminded of Dr. Tournier and his inspiring chat by the fire when I saw a photo recently . . . of myself! Frankly, it was a surreal moment as I realized that I am now the old man! As pastors frequently gather with me for in-depth conversations, they often express the same longing for understanding that I have had. It is in these reflective settings that we each take turns unpacking our stories, and we often remind each other of the importance and power of deep listening. We typically share the quote already mentioned from another esteemed psychiatrist, Dr. Karl Menninger: "Listening is a magnetic and strange thing, a creative force. The friends who listen to us are the ones we move toward. When [we feel] we are listened to, it creates us, makes us unfold and expand."

We all have a longing to be listened to and accepted. When that happens, there is often a surprising bonding that happens. At first I didn't understand when someone not all that much younger than I would refer to me as a sort of spiritual father. I sometimes naively assumed they were just teasing me about my age and hair color. Well, now that I have even less hair, and what little I have is gray, I'm beginning to appreciate what they were really communicating.

Spiritual fathering is not about age but about influence. It's not about a title but a relationship, not so much about bi-ology but more about bonding. We all have a few who fit this definition, though we may never have actually honored them by sharing our high esteem for them.

Clearly, there are times when we need to acknowledge and honor those who God has used to help shape our souls.

- "For even if you had ten thousand others to teach you about Christ, you have only one spiritual father. For I became your father in Christ Jesus when I preached the Good News to you. So I urge you to imitate me" (1 Corinthians 4:15–16).

- "And you know that we treated each of you as a father treats his own children. We pleaded with you, encouraged you, and urged you to live your lives in a way that God would consider worthy. For he called you to share in his Kingdom and glory" (1 Thessalonians 2:11–12).

Francis Chan said, "You can walk away from a belief system but not a father." The relationship we each have with our imperfect father is profound. I was privileged to have a strong relationship with my father; however, sadly, many have had painful and even terrible ones. That's what has led several to tell me, "You are the closest thing to a father in my life," or "You are the father I always wanted to have," or "You are like a spiritual father to me."

Spiritual parentage is not about perfection but personal trust; therefore, it carries both surprising privileges and special responsibilities. On the *privilege* side I am entrusted with private information and given surprising freedom to guide and even to challenge. On the *responsibility* side I am increasingly aware that I must take special care with my words. I'm regularly reminded that the toughest of men can have the tenderest of hearts!

We are all blessed with life-enriching relationships. None of us are spiritual orphans. Someone has influenced us, shaped us, and encouraged us in our spiritual journey, and a few of them still do. When these people come to mind, it should prompt us both to honor them and to thank God for them. Maybe even apologize to them!

A few years ago, as soon as my plane landed back in Denver after a work trip, I received a surprising text message from a former associate. To put it kindly, his ministry with our church did not end well. After considerable reflection he wrote this:

> I'm in a season of life and ministry where I'm seeking to learn everything I can about honor, and instill it into my life at a deep level. There's a story where Jesus goes home to Nazareth after his amazing line of miracles. Because it's home he is not given the honor he's worthy of, and it actually binds his power.
>
> Instead of making lame walk and blind see, he heals a few headaches. I am convinced that my lack of showing honor to you bound the power of God at some level. I want you to know how heartbroken and repentant I am for failing your leadership in this way. I ask for your forgiveness and pray God's blessing on you and your ministry.
>
> Sorry this is so out of the blue, and likely very strange.

I responded immediately. "My plane has just landed in Denver. Your heartfelt and thoughtful apology is deeply appreciated. I am on a special kind of Rocky Mountain high as a result! Blessings, on your head and heart."

Later the two of us had a lengthy conversation unpacking more of what prompted this apology. While I've been the recipient of many honors and kind words over the years, I have never received such a stunning and enlightening apology. This humble expression of remorse and honoring deeply blessed me. I'm certain it did the same for him.

So who are the ones you might need to honor? We've all been blessed by spiritual fathers and mothers, leaders and influencers, but do they know it? Whom might you long to have an unhindered conversation with? Whom might you need to bare your soul with?

THE SECRET SAUCE OF TRANSFORMATION

Everyone is interested in the secret sauce of transformation.

How is it that while some merely go through life, others *grow* through life—as well as grow through leadership? Some have tried to summarize it with the following formula:

Change of Place + Change of Pace = Change of Perspective

I love that, but I would suggest one more element. Change of perspective almost always happens in community, that is, with other people who sharpen and deepen us.

Change of Place + Change of Pace + *Change of People* =
Change in Perspective

Let's take a closer look at the elements in this recipe for
transformation.

"Change of Place" involves moving to an actual location.

That might be a vacation getaway, your favorite coffee shop,
or simply the leather recliner in your own home. For groups
like the ones I have enjoyed, that place often happened to be a
semiannual retreat on the holy ground of a beautiful mountain
home in Colorado.

"Change of Pace" involves deliberately choosing to be still.

Some people I know actually fear stillness. They allow their
days to be filled with noise from beginning to end. In our semiannual retreats together with a handful of others, we regularly
"take two." That's the simple discipline of periodically enjoying
two minutes of silence even as we sit in a circle of other highly
verbal leaders.

**"Change of People" involves allowing yourself to enter into
the inner worlds of others and allowing them to enter into
your own.**

That's a scary experience for some, and it requires courage.
As Brené Brown has written, "The root of the word courage is

cor—the Latin word for heart. In one of its earliest forms the word *courage* had a very different definition than it does today. Courage originally meant 'To speak one's mind by telling all one's heart."[18] Few of us need to be surrounded by more people; we need to encircle ourselves with the right people—courageous people.

The truth is, we were designed for more than endless frenetic activity and countless casual interactions. We were created to enjoy life in community. Not just surface interactions but in-depth connections. These sorts of experiences almost only happen intentionally. Someone has to seek them and facilitate them. And that person could be you!

LIFE-ENRICHING RELATIONSHIPS ARE LIFE-CHANGING

Your life will never be happier or healthier than the soul care circle of friends who surround you. In the Journal of Happiness Studies, researchers studied the differences between very happy people and those less happy. What they found was not a difference in their career success, personal health, IQ, or even attractiveness. The difference was entirely due to the presence or absence of life-enriching relationships.

Robert Putnam writes, "The single most common finding from a half-century's research on life satisfaction, not only in the U.S. but around the world, is that happiness is best predicted by the breadth and depth of one's social connections."[19]

Quality connections don't just happen. You are where you are relationally right now because of relational seeds you have sown or failed to sow. The psalmist said, "I will search for faithful people to be my companions" (Psalm 101:6). This means that we must take initiative both in the acquisition of good friendships and in the maintenance of them.

Relationships require work, creative work. We grow best with those we invest in and make time to be with. We gain insights and catch attitudes from those we allow to surround us. We must be willing to make choices and do the work to achieve the life-enriching relationships we desire.

REFLECTION QUESTIONS

Do the people at your "table of influence" know the role they play in your life?

How would you describe your life-giving rhythms, both of activity and relationship?

Who might be in the category of a spiritual parent for you?

CHAPTER 4

CULTIVATE STRONG RELATIONSHIPS

"THERE CAN BE NO VULNERABILITY WITHOUT RISK; THERE CAN BE NO COMMUNITY WITHOUT VULNERABILITY; THERE CAN BE NO PEACE, AND ULTIMATELY NO LIFE, WITHOUT COMMUNITY."

—M. SCOTT PECK

Gordon MacDonald shares a story about a rabbi sitting in his study when interrupted by a knock on the door. It was one of his students who simply wanted to tell him how much he loved him.

The rabbi put down his book and looked over his glasses and asked, "What hurts me?"

The boy was speechless. Finally he responded, "I don't know."

"How can you say that you love me if you don't know what hurts me?" the wise rabbi responded.

So who knows what hurts you? Who knows something about your heartaches and your soul stress?

Soul work is not only *slow* work; soul work is *shared* work. However, all relationships aren't created equal, nor do they all carry the same level of responsibility for disclosure.

STRONG RELATIONSHIPS REQUIRE AUTHENTICITY

Responsible, authentic connection is not "one size fits all." While it's important to be authentic with everyone, there are levels we must consider, beginning with honesty and progressively moving to vulnerability. However, that progression only happens as trust increases. As trust goes up, vulnerability goes up. As trust goes down, vulnerability goes down.

Honesty with all is foundational. But being a truth teller doesn't mean that everyone has the right to know everything that others know. All God-honoring relationships begin with honesty; it's an essential element of authenticity. Honesty means telling the truth. However, honesty doesn't mean telling the whole truth to the whole wide world or even to everyone in the neighborhood or church lobby. Honesty with all and kindness to all is good for us all. That's the foundation on which all authentic relationships are founded.

Transparency builds on the foundation of honesty. It comes after we've grown to trust the credentials and character of a person. This happens best within smaller groups. That's the space where we open up about some of the personal struggles of our lives knowing that we're only as sick as our secrets. Yet our most embarrassing secrets are reserved for our most time-tested friendships and the most confidential settings.

THE 3 LEVELS OF AUTHENTICITY

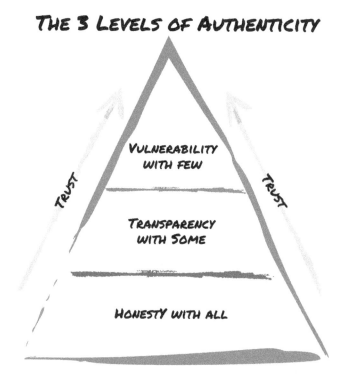

Vulnerability happens in the tightest of relationships and the smallest of circles. That's when we decide to come out of hiding and share the things that may have haunted us for years. Or it might be sharing our greatest pain or our deepest fears. It's telling a colleague about a betrayal or unloading our anxiety about the future. These relationships are rare and must be cultivated. They don't happen accidentally; they happen intentionally.

There are many valid reasons for relational caution. Too many have faced betrayal, abandonment, or personal judgment. Believe it or not, even Jesus was cautious in friendship. "But Jesus didn't trust them, because he knew all about people. No one needed to tell him about human nature" (John 2:24–25). As President Ronald Reagan famously said, "Trust but verify!" That's wise advice not just in foreign affairs but also in personal relationships!

I once built a fence with my father-in-law. My wife and I lived on a corner lot with our three active little kids. So even though money was extremely tight, I scraped enough together to buy the lumber and built a sturdy fence to keep our rambunctious ones in the yard. It took a few days of hard labor, but we completed it together—one board at a time!

One board at a time is how both fences and friendships are built. It takes a long time, but sturdy fences and friendships are worth it. As Kenny Rogers once said, "You can't go out and make old friends; you either have them or you don't!"

Quality friendships and deep relationships require the risk of trust. Trust is like a picket fence—it can come down quickly but can only be rebuilt slowly, if at all.

Sadly, shattered relationships are all too common, even among believers. Sooner or later, all human relationships will be stress tested. Over time, flaws will always be revealed.

That's why we're told in John 2:24 (NIV), "But Jesus would not entrust himself to them, for he knew all people." Oswald Chambers wisely said, "Never trust anything but the grace of God in yourself or in anyone else."

Only God can be God to us, worthy of the weight of our absolute eternal trust. This is the point of Psalm 91:2: "This I declare about the LORD: He alone is my refuge, my place of safety; he is my God, and I trust him." No one but God is capable of perfection, and He is the only rock we can rely on 24-7 both for now and forever.

No one else will always be perfect, even those who sincerely seek to be!

We all take turns letting people down. Sometimes it's just an inadvertent oversight; other times it might be a matter of deliberate betrayal. In his masterful book *Let's Talk About Ministry Burnout*, Dr. Wes Beavis enlightened me on the science of betrayal by quoting the work of psychiatrist Dr. Daniel Siegel. Did you know that the brain groups the pain of betrayal in the same category as the pain of a broken bone or root canal? He says, "So, when betrayal happens, your brain processes it as trauma—as if a car door was slammed on your fingers. Betrayal is painful and science backs that up in the way the brain deals with it."[20]

Imperfections are inevitable. However, there's a big difference between the relational stress that comes from a simple oversight—such as "Oops, I forgot to return your call!"—and an entrenched pattern of self-protection or deceit, or out right rejection and betrayal.

Someone once said to me, "I've lied to you for ten years, but I will never lie to you again." What if a fellow believer severely violated your trust and, after being discovered, said that to you? How would you respond? While you would sincerely offer forgiveness and wish the brother or sister well, would you be quick to fully trust him again?

We've all had our share of relational disappointments and trust-shattering experiences. I identified with Aaron Brockett, lead pastor of Traders Point Christian Church in Indianapolis, when he said in a podcast, "I have at times been too enamored by someone's gifts and therefore blinded to their lack of character."[21]

We've all learned the hard way that relationships can only be built, or rebuilt, slowly. Trust must be earned. As King David wrote, "I will search for faithful people to be my companions" (Psalm 101:6).

Relationships only grow at the speed of trust. The best ones are devoid of both self-promotion and self-protection.

Five years ago I was in a covenant group that soon went deep. While we all knew each other prior, our relationships grew far beyond anything we had experienced together before. They reached the point where we had no secrets.

We breathed the rare air of trust. One of the guys closed our three-year soul care journey by saying, "I can't believe it took me well into my sixties to finally experience something like this!"

It's never too soon—and it's never too late—to begin, or to begin again, building relationships of trust, one board at a time.

We ought to be cautious with close relationships because trust is earned. Yet over time we come to recognize those who God has sent our way to enrich and enlighten us. None of us have all spiritual gifts within us; however, the good news from Psalm 23 is that the Lord is our Good Shepherd and He promises to give us everything we need!

STRONG RELATIONSHIPS REQUIRE DEVOTION

Once again, you can't lead anyone to where you have never been or are not going yourself! The journey of transformation is a lifelong journey, and it is also a shared one.

As the African proverb says, "If you want to go fast, go *alone*; if you want to go far, go *together!*" Christianity is all about community; therefore, Christian leadership and discipleship are all about building and enjoying community as well.

One of the keys to understanding the community of the early church is an often overlooked word in our culture—the word *devoted*. In our culture few are devoted to much of anything or anyone beyond themselves. We see that in the mobility of the culture at large, the breakdown of the family, the disintegration of communities, and even the lack of loyalty to local congregations.

Congregations are increasingly composed of mere attenders and occasional consumers. Seldom does anyone talk about their local church as their church home. Certainly not as the place where they *belong*. Instead, it's casually referenced as the place where they currently go.

Even as leaders when we wonder about the people we haven't seen for a while, we will ask, "Where are they *going* now?" By contrast the model of the New Testament church was not merely *going* but *belonging* to a devoted community: "They devoted themselves to . . . the *fellowship* . . . . And all who believed were *together* and *had all things in common. . . . they received their food with glad and generous hearts, praising God and having favor with all the people*" (Acts 2:42–47 ESV, emphasis mine).

In the Greek language, the word *koinonia* means "community," and community is the key to fullness of life. The Father, Son, and Spirit were in perfect community before the beginning of time. We have been redeemed to enjoy community with the Lord and His people for both time and eternity.

This is why the phrase "one another" appears fifty-nine times in the Scriptures.

- We're to love one another (1 John 3:11).
- We're to instruct one another (Romans 15:14).
- We're to encourage one another (1 Thessalonians 5:11).
- We're to spur one another to good works (Hebrews 10:24).
- We're to rejoice and weep with one another (Romans 12:15).

- We're to forgive one another (Ephesians 4:32).
- We're to confess our faults to one another (James 5:16).
- We're to pray for one another (James 5:16).

Clearly we are better together. We belong together as partners with Christ and with one another. In his personal letter to the church in Philippi, the apostle Paul repeatedly refers to the leaders and others as partners. Then several times he even uses the term *yokefellows*.

Where did Paul get this word? He got it from Jesus. Jesus commanded, "Take my yoke upon you" (Matthew 11:29). We voluntarily bow before our Lord. We allow him to put his yoke on us. Christ's yoke represents his authority, his character, his mission.

Christ's yoke binds us all together as we pull in the same direction. We will only be as strong as the team that we are yoked and united with. It is a synergistic principle that can be illustrated this way:

In a horse-pulling contest up in Canada, the finest work-horses of the community were brought in and the bets were placed. The first-place horse won the day pulling nine thousand pounds, and the one in second place was close behind with just under that amount. Then someone got the bright idea, what would happen if the horses were teamed up and pulling together? What then?

The people were intrigued and excited, so the bets were placed and the event was on. To everyone's amazement the two horses that had earlier pulled nine thousand pounds each, now working together, pulled thirty thousand pounds!

Since when does nine plus nine equal thirty? Since always. It's the synergistic principle—the sum is greater than that of its individual parts!

In the ultimate sense, it's not just what you do, where you go, or how much you accomplish in life. It's about who you go with. Might God be calling you to be a catalyst for deeper community? Could there be a new community opportunity with your name on it?

Consider this: what if some of the best friends you've ever had, you have yet to meet? Now, for some reading this, community is scary. I get that. I'll let you in on a secret. Every time I catalyze another group, I wonder if it's going to work! Yet every time I face my fear and work to bring others together, God shows up in the middle of it!

STRONG RELATIONSHIPS REQUIRE INTENTIONALITY

Here's what we know from decades of church programming: church programs don't produce transformation. Here's what we do know from the model of Jesus: transformation happens on purpose, over time, and in community.

- *On Purpose*   - *Over Time*

Transformation

- *In Community*

- On Purpose
- Over Time
- In Community

This is why intentional small groups like covenant groups are so impactful. Soul care isn't a technique but a disciplined art requiring facilitation. Remember: if it's not led, it won't last. A life-enriching soul care circle requires all of the following:

- Consistency
- Confidentiality
- Candor
- Care-*full*-ness

Transformation can't be reduced to a rigid formula. Not even with a helpful resource or the latest best-selling book of Bible-based devotions. What we all need is to slow down and embrace a process. A process that happens on purpose, over time, and in community.

David Benner has written a profound book entitled *Sacred Companions: The Gift of Spiritual Friendship and Direction*. He says, "The hunger for connection is one of the most fundamental desires of the human heart. . . . In the core of our being we yearn for intimacy. We want people to share our lives. We want soul friends. . . . Paradoxically, however, what we most deeply long for we also fear."[22]

Benner calls these special allies "sacred companions" or "spiritual friends." He says, "If you are making significant progress on the transformational journey of Christian spirituality, you have one or more friendships that support that journey. If you do not, you are not. It's that simple."[23]

Everyone agrees that cultivating these kinds of deep relationships is vital; therefore, most plan to do it . . . next year. My mission is to challenge people to make *next year* happen *this year*!

Dwight L. Moody once said, "Preparation for old age should not begin later than one's teens. A life which is empty of purpose until 65 will not suddenly become filled on retirement."

Soul-enriching connections can't happen soon enough. We all need a vital few who know us well.

And we need them now.

Might your life be just one call or email away from being better? Yes, of course! There's no better time than now to take some relational initiative. So, who do you know who might be ready and willing to enrich you and to be enriched by you?

Healthy and fulfilling relationships are essential to a healthy and fulfilling life!

STRONG RELATIONSHIPS REQUIRE TIME

Spiritual growth, as with physical growth, takes time. In M. Robert Mulholland's classic book *Invitation to a Journey: A Road Map for Spiritual Transformation,* I found this insightful definition: "Spiritual formation is a process of being formed in the image of Christ for the sake of others."[24] In other words, growth doesn't happen overnight; it only happens over time.

I heard Paul Young, author of *The Shack,* say that he couldn't have written that remarkable story (which was his own story of abuse) until after the age of fifty. He talked about the need to move beyond the false self. The healthy soul requires setting aside both *self-promotion* and *self-protection.* For Paul Young, reaching that point required the hard work of intensive conversation and deep community. The same will be true for all who truly desire transformation of the heart.

Dallas Willard once advised John Ortberg, "You must ruthlessly eliminate hurry from your life." In *The Life You've Always Wanted,* Ortberg tells of a friend who also received a similar insight from Dallas. Dallas asked Bill, "If you had one word to describe Jesus, what would it be?" Various words were mentioned, such as teacher, Lord, and compassionate. Then Dallas offered his own word. It was simply *relaxed*.[25]

I've got a long way to grow in becoming more like Jesus. As Milton once warned, "Do not let Satan tempt you to be in a hurry about anything."

Many years ago Samuel Chadwick wrote, "Hurry is the death of prayer." To that I would add, hurry is the death of depth. It's been observed that it takes an average of seven minutes to go deep; however, we are interrupted every three minutes!

When was the last time you enjoyed a relaxed and unhurried face-to-face conversation with someone you value and trust? Often when I ask these questions, I see a bit of sadness sweep across a face as the person comes to grips with the dearth of heartfelt and soul-enriching relationships in their life.

During the COVID closures, countless gatherings were cancelled. One leader said, "I told my wife I'm not sure I can handle another year merely connecting via Zoom. I miss being with people!" It's the same cry of the heart we read in 3 John 14: "For I hope to see you soon, and then we will talk face to face."

Lingering conversations are essential for life transformation and relational fulfillment.

STRONG RELATIONSHIPS REQUIRE CULTIVATION

Relationships of quality must be cultivated. This was confirmed in *The Power of Moments: Why Certain Experiences Have*

Extraordinary Impact by Chip and Dan Heath.[26] The authors cite a study in which college students in a psychology class volunteered to be paired up with strangers.

Each pair of students was given several dozen questions to pull out of an envelope. The exercise was divided into three rounds of fifteen minutes each. At the end of the forty-five-minute experiment they took a survey on the intimacy of their relationships with those closest to them. What amazed the research team is that after the experiment 30 percent of the students now felt as close to a stranger as to those in the most intimate relationships of their lives! That was after just forty-five minutes!

It's been said that the key is the question! If that's true, imagine asking thirty-six exploratory questions. The questions were developed by a team of researchers who had spent decades researching how relationships of connection and love are formed. One key pattern is escalating reciprocity, which refers to how close relationships progress and are sustained.

Here are my favorites, each of which I field tested with my own wife. Amazingly, a few of these led to a few discoveries for me even after fifty years together!

Set 1

- Given the choice of anyone in the world, whom would you want as a dinner guest?

- What would constitute a "perfect" day for you?
- If you could wake up tomorrow having gained any one quality or ability, what would it be?

Set 2

- What is the greatest accomplishment of your life?
- What is your most treasured memory?
- What is your most terrible memory?

Set 3

- Share with your partner an embarrassing moment in your life.
- If you were to die this evening with no opportunity to communicate with anyone, what would you most regret not having told someone? Why haven't you told them yet?
- Your house, containing everything you own, catches fire. After saving your loved ones and pets, you have time to safely make a final dash to save any one item. What would it be? Why?

A few years ago my word for the year was *moments.* That prompted me sometimes to ask friends, "If this were the last moment we ever had together, is there anything we have yet to say that ought to be said?" Wow, did that elicit some interesting conversation.

I realized after one of my retreats that I had been racing the clock. One of the reasons I was sometimes pushing so hard was rooted in my concern that I cover everything, just in case it might be my last opportunity. When I told my wife, she quickly said, "If this were the last moment, better it be a relaxed moment."

We all know what it is to rush through life, missing the most significant moments while they are taking place. Soul work is slow work.

Consider this: the present moment may be the divine moment!

REFLECTION QUESTIONS

Has it been more challenging for you to set aside self-promotion or self-protection?

How might you have been recently wounded by a toxic person or blessed by a safe one?

Would you describe yourself as more hurried or more relaxed?

CHAPTER 5

LEARN THE RHYTHMS OF GRACE

"THIS IS WHAT THE LORD SAYS: 'STOP AT THE CROSSROADS AND LOOK AROUND. ASK FOR THE OLD, GODLY WAY, AND WALK IN IT. TRAVEL ITS PATH, AND YOU WILL FIND REST FOR YOUR SOULS.'"

—JEREMIAH 6:16

True confession.

I have been an acceptance addict and I've paid a high price. The desire for acceptance has at times driven me to ridiculous levels of performance through people pleasing and approval seeking. I haven't wanted to disappoint anyone. I've wanted everyone to be happy with me and admire my efforts to serve them and others. I've even sacrificed my family, free time, and health in the service of others.

Not everything I've done in ministry leadership has always been completely noble. In my early years of ministry I spent too many evenings visiting the families of the church rather than enjoying my own. I was sometimes afraid to answer the phone when at home for fear of criticism that I should have been serving the church. For too many years and in too many ways, I have been driven and burdened in my pursuit of serving and pleasing God's people.

This all came crashing down on me at a men's retreat a few years ago. I had no idea what I was getting into when shortly after I arrived one of the hosts privately interviewed me, asking a soul-searching question.

"What do you want to work on while you are here?"

I didn't expect such a serious question, so I suddenly made an embarrassing admission.

"I want to feel more of the love and acceptance of God."

Sometimes I amaze even myself by what I hear myself say! In that moment, though it was true, it sounded immature and needy, especially for a sixty-six-year-old, longtime Christian leader.

Then it got worse. I was given a large piece of paper and colorful markers like I was a little kid and asked to draw something representing how I felt. At first it frustrated and irritated me. I had no clue what to draw when suddenly an image clearly came to mind. It's one cemented in my mind since I see it every day on my desk.

Some years ago I received a special award along with the gift of a beautiful item made of marble and crystal. It depicted a man pushing a huge boulder up a steep hill. Many of you will recall the Greek myth of Sisyphus and how he was condemned to push a boulder up a hill, and each time he got near the top, the boulder came rolling back down the hill again.

As soon as I opened the box and saw the figure, it resonated with me. That's how I felt. I had to keep pushing the heavy burdens of life or else they would crush me. I couldn't cease. I couldn't stop. I couldn't relax. I had to keep pushing.

Now, some of this is rooted in the old Protestant work ethic and definitely in my family of origin. I grew up in a strong Christian home, but times were tough. My dad always feared losing his job and visibly carried the weight of that. My mom worried about my dad's job and everything else as well. I grew up breathing the air of high anxiety. The message I internalized was I could never worry enough or work enough. I could never truly cease or stop or relax.

The boulder for me was the unrelenting pressure to perform. As a result of the boulder I often blamed myself for not being good enough or working hard enough. I even blamed my wife and a few others for not understanding me or supporting me enough. Ultimately, I blamed God for giving me such a heavy burden to push.

It's been said that blame seems hardwired into most of us. It's a quick way to discharge pain. Well, that doesn't excuse it, but it does help to explain it. I was pushing a ton of emotional pain as I struggled with my performance not being enough.

What finally came together for me was that the boulder of performance was the crushing weight that God never intended for me to bear. In reality, that boulder, representing all the brokenness and sin of my life and the lives of those around me, actually was the crushing weight that fell on Christ. Isaiah 53 says that "he was pierced for our rebellion, crushed for our sins," and "it was the LORD's good plan to crush him and cause him grief" (Isaiah 53:5, 10).

That's when the image I drew became complete, and at the retreat I pictured a crucifix under the massive boulder. In that moment as I looked at it, I realized that my achievement efforts would never be enough to make me acceptable to God. Only Christ could accomplish that on the cross. That's what He died to complete.

This was a profound experience for me. As I've shared it with a few others, I've discovered that it often powerfully resonates with them too. I'm learning that I'm not alone in feeling that I am often pushing an impossible weight uphill.

WHAT IS YOUR PERFORMANCE BOULDER?

One of my close friends is a wealth manager. He shared how his "performance boulder" represents a couple hundred investment portfolios that he manages for his clients. He daily lives with the angst that if he advises everyone to stay in the market when it dives, his clients could take a beating. On the other hand, if he cautiously advises his clients to take a conservative approach and hold heavy cash positions when the market soars, he fails them.

After Dave shared this picture with his wife, Angela, she said, "Well, Dave, my portfolio is the welfare of our daughters. If they're not doing well, I'm not doing well!" Everyone has some sort of portfolio of concern. Everyone has a boulder of some sort they are pushing.

PUSHING THE BOULDER

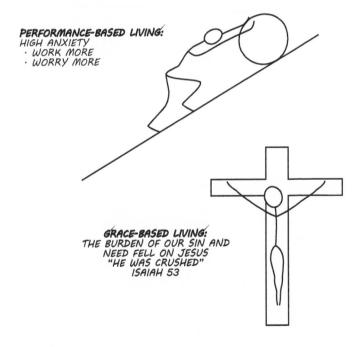

PERFORMANCE-BASED LIVING:
HIGH ANXIETY
· WORK MORE
· WORRY MORE

GRACE-BASED LIVING:
THE BURDEN OF OUR SIN AND
NEED FELL ON JESUS
"HE WAS CRUSHED"
ISAIAH 53

In my first full-time ministry the leaders actually wrote my performance boulder into the by-laws. Six couples called me to lead a church plant after they had split from another church over a conflict with the minister. They decided that the leader of the new church (me) would have to perform well in order to remain.

It was determined that an annual congregational vote of approval would be required. A two-thirds vote! Now, every new pastor soon realizes that the likelihood of keeping an entire congregation happy at the same time is impossible. Even the vast majority. This meant that in addition to seeing new people quickly added to the church, I also needed to please the existing people. Both were essential to pay the bills and to keep my job.

Their well-intended action just reinforced the worst of my performance anxieties. While the church grew well, it came at a high price. It wasn't well with my soul. I worked nonstop. I felt it was my calling to be a high-performance ministry machine. I wasn't concerned about losing my salvation, but I was concerned about losing my job!

One of the elders gave me a humorous sign for my office: "Around here I have a very responsible position—every time anything goes wrong, I'm responsible!" They all laughed about it. I internalized it!

Every leader feels at times that he is pushing something uphill. Those who score as Threes, called Achievers, on the Enneagram especially resonate with this.

Those with a profile like mine get a ton done and take pride in doing so. In the book *The Road Back to You,* I clearly saw myself. "Early in life Threes [people like me] pick up the wounding message 'You are what you do.' As a result they become high-performance achievement machines, striving to excel and be acknowledged for their accomplishments because they constitute the basis of their identity."[27]

Tyler Zach shares many helpful insights in his book *The Gospel for Achievers.* "Do you find it frustrating when you are unable to accomplish all that you want to get done? While 'Achievers' are able to accomplish much, they rarely are satisfied with the results, so they chase for contentment and the hope for rest from labor can seem as far as the horizon."[28]

That same little book reminded me that our tombstone is not likely to record our accomplishments. It actually forced me to reflect on my own tombstone. I wrote what I most long to hear: "Well done, good and faithful servant."

The reality is that most people will summarize our lives in one sentence . . . or less! That's beyond sobering since we would all like to be remembered for far more. That's especially true for those of us specializing in living life with a long to-do list every day.

This is dangerous territory. While people like me may get a lot done and take pride in the doing of it, in our relentless pushing we often lose our footing. Pushing others leads to relational breakdowns. Pushing ourselves leads to personal burnout. I know about both.

Setting high performance standards for our staff didn't always inspire them. It annoyed and frustrated them. Setting ever higher expectations for myself often elevated my own anxieties about not measuring up.

I just couldn't stop achieving more or worrying that I wasn't. At one point my physician challenged me.

He said, "When are you going to do something about the stress you are carrying? This isn't good for you!"

To which I snarkily replied, "Just because you got up on the wrong side of the bed, why are you taking it out on me?"

He didn't laugh that off, but instead said, "I love you and I want the best for you and this isn't it."

Not long after, I was diagnosed with a stress fracture. My wife insisted that I have a bone density test. The doctors agreed with my wife, as most people eventually do, and discovered that I also had severe osteoporosis in much of my body. Do you know who typically gets that? Heavy smokers, drinkers, and postmenopausal octogenarians! I was none of the above. However, I later learned from the book *The HeartMath Solution* that the stress hormone cortisol depletes calcium from the bones and is a precursor to osteoporosis. In addition, "Chronically elevated levels of cortisol have been shown to impair immune function, reduce glucose utilization, increase bone loss and promote osteoporosis, reduce muscle mass, inhibit skin growth and regeneration, increase fat accumulation (especially around the waist and hips), impair memory and learning and destroy brain cells."[29]

I can identify with all of the above, and that's why I became convicted to making a change. For years, when it came to stress, I prided myself on being a "power lifter." Many wondered how I carried so much responsibility so well. Frankly, so did I. I wondered how I was getting away with my addiction to performance. Well, I didn't get away with it.

FLOORED BY GRACE—LITERALLY

At the Men at the Cross retreat this became clear to me when I literally ended up on the floor. After my new friends heard some of my story, they surprised me with an intervention. I was blindfolded and carefully laid on what I quickly realized was a large wooden cross. One by one stones were placed on my back. The stones each had words written on them, some of them my own performance words. As the stones piled up, my emotions did as well. Suddenly I was heaving with tears, sobbing uncontrollably with snot flowing freely.

The wise men around and over me let the emotions run their course. Then each took a turn removing the stones. As they did, they blessed me with liberating words of acceptance.
They repeatedly reminded me of the grace of Jesus and His acceptance of me. An acceptance not based on my performance but on His!

There's an old hymn by James Proctor, which I only recently discovered, entitled "It is Finished." The words that especially gripped and convicted me were, "Lay your deadly doing down—down at Jesus' feet. Stand in him alone, gloriously complete."

From that day on the floor, I have often worn a crucifix. Not a cross, a crucifix. One just like my Roman Catholic childhood buddies used to wear or have hanging from their rearview mirrors back in Chicago. Believe it or not, I once thought it was almost heretical for good Protestant kids like me to revere a crucifix. After all, we don't worship a dead hero but a living Lord! That's certainly true; however, now the crucifix reminds me that the position of Savior has been taken!

I now understand at a deeper level than ever that I am loved apart from what I do. I am accepted apart from how I perform. I am forgiven and blame free apart from anything I deserve. It's all because of what Christ has done for me.

Everything comes back to what Christ did on the cross. Jesus came to declare that through faith in Him we are accepted by God. As clearly recorded in John 6:29, "This is the only work God wants from you: Believe in the one he has sent." And as the apostle Paul, a former high-performance Pharisee, shared, "Everyone who believes in him is made right in God's sight—something the Law of Moses could never do" (Acts 13:39).

How is it that something so frequently repeated in Scripture is so often forgotten by people who daily read it! It has something to do with our failure to internalize truth. We all struggle with applying our theology. That's why I have to keep reminding myself that grace is not opposed to effort; grace is opposed to earning. Working and serving can be noble and God honoring when it is done *with* God and not merely *for* pleasing either God or people.

I now see that love is acceptance. For reasons I can't fully explain, I was prompted to paraphrase this familiar passage on love by simply inserting the word *accept, accepted,* or *acceptance* every time love was referenced. When I did that, the text went from black words on a white page to words leaping off the page. Here it is from 1 John 4:7–12:

> Dear friends, let us continue to *accept* one another, for *acceptance* comes from God. Anyone who *accepts* is a child of God and knows God. But anyone who does not *accept* does not know God, for God is *acceptance.*

> God showed how much he *accepted* us by sending his one and only Son into the world so that we might have eternal life through him. This is real *acceptance*—not that we *accepted* God, but that he *accepted* us and sent his Son as a sacrifice to take away our sins.

> Dear friends, since God *accepted* us that much, we surely ought to *accept* each other. No one has ever seen God. But if we *accept* each other, God lives in us, and his *acceptance* is brought to full expression in us.

I dare you to read that passage with the *acceptance* words again out loud—to someone you love! It's been said that no one ever changes unless someone accepts him first! Acceptance is the gift God gives us through Jesus, and acceptance is the gift we give to others through the grace given to us. Here are the steps:

1. Accept that you are totally accepted, not by your performance but by Christ's.
2. Celebrate the gift of God's acceptance by admitting your desperate need for His grace.
3. Accept the imperfections of others close to you, just as you would like them to accept yours.

EMBRACE GRACE SO YOU CAN GIVE GRACE

I've been addicted to earning acceptance—now, by God's grace I'm becoming devoted to *extending* acceptance. The reality is that when I feel accepted I want acceptance to flow out of me—especially to others closest to me. No doubt that's true for you as well.

When we internalize the good news of grace, applying it first to ourselves, it changes us. As the psalmist said, "I heard an unknown voice say, 'Now I will take the load from your shoulders; I will free your hands from their heavy tasks. You cried to me in trouble, and I saved you" (Psalm 81:5–7).

It's been said, that which is the most personal becomes the most universal. And recent brain research shows that using feeling words creates connections. One of the key abilities of the most successful leaders in business and ministry is the capacity to know what they and others feel in the moment.

As I have shared my personal performance story using feeling words such as "stress fracture" and "crushed," many have identified. Some have even started wearing a crucifix themselves as a reminder that the ultimate achievement is Christ's, not ours. Our need is to daily depend on the Lover of our soul for His strength. Others have shared the message with their families as they personally blessed them. After one of the young pastors in a covenant group shared it with his wife, she later surprised him with a special Father's Day gift. It was a handcrafted plaque of a cross with the words "The position of Savior has been taken—Jesus is enough!"

How might this be God's message to you? Shortly after my personal breakdown leading to a breakthrough of acceptance, I found a helpful book. We encourage all of our groups to use it, and it can be read in full in only forty-nine minutes.

The book is *One Word That Will Change Your Life* by Dan Britton, Jimmy Page, and Jon Gordon.[30]

The authors contend that goal setting rarely works; however, simply focusing on one word does. This got my attention and led me into a process to identify God's one word for me to focus on during the entire year.

It wasn't hard; in fact, I've been following that pattern for the last seven years. It won't surprise you that the first year my word was acceptance! Then came these: Enjoy. Flow. Surrounded. Moments. Relax. Rhythm.

The authors suggest three questions to discover God's one word:

- What do you need?
- What's in your way?
- What needs to go?

What do I most need to focus on right now?

- Right now it's *rhythm*: learning to enjoy the unforced rhythms of grace—reflectively, relationally, and recreationally.

What's in my way?

- Right now it's my propensity for being performance driven and pushing too hard.

What needs to go?

- Right now it's my activity addiction and "hurry sickness."

ARE YOU READY TO DANCE?

I really enjoyed another refreshing book by Ruth Haley Barton called *Sacred Rhythms: Arranging Our Lives for Spiritual Transformation.*

She prefers the language of rhythm. I strongly resonate with that as well.

Much to my wife's disappointment, I don't have the natural rhythm of movement required for dancing. However, I am capable of learning and developing rhythms for soul-enriching living. After years of feeling like I was often "pushing a boulder uphill," I'm now growing in what Eugene Peterson calls "the unforced rhythms of grace."

> "Are you tired? Worn out? Burned out on religion? Come to me. Get away with me and you'll recover your life. I'll show you how to take a real rest. Walk with me and work with me—watch how I do it. Learn the unforced rhythms of grace. I won't lay anything heavy or ill-fitting on you. Keep company with me and you'll learn to live freely and lightly." (Matthew 11:28–30 MSG)

I'm discovering that just as my life will be no richer than my relationships, it's also true that my life will be no richer than my rhythms! Truth be told, I quickly feel out of whack and even out of sorts without my life-giving rhythms.

In the business world many say, "Your systems are perfectly designed to get you what you are getting!" What if we put it this way: "Your rhythms are perfectly designed to get you what you are getting!"

When I shared that with one of my previous covenant groups as we reconnected on a Zoom call, a young leader said, "Now I realize what's happening with me. Ever since the current crisis began, I stopped the life-giving rhythm of journaling and more. I'm now paying the price!"

Are you rhythmically thriving or merely surviving? I've been led to the land of well-being in at least three ways: reflectively, relationally, and recreationally. These are the three areas of my life that consistently produce the greatest return on investment for me.

- Reflectively: My reflective rhythms ground me in God's daily mercies. I love to begin each day slowly soaking in God's presence, listening for His leading and seeking His prompting.

- Relationally: My relational rhythms connect me with the gift of disciplined community. I daily seek to connect with life-enhancing people who sharpen, deepen, resource, and connect me.

- Recreationally: My recreational rhythms invigorate me in body, mind, and spirit with God's creation. Daily exercise isn't an interruption in my life; it's an enhancement.

Thriving is all about well-being. King David once prayed, "The Lord be exalted, who delights in the well-being of his servant" (Psalm 35:27 NIV). Frankly, too many times my "stinkin' thinkin'" and substandard theology have led me to patterns that were far from conducive to improving my well-being.

- Reflectively: I once determined to read the entire Bible out loud over the course of a year. That drained me more than blessed me.

- Relationally: I once committed to a schedule that included both evening appointments and early morning meetings. Burning the candle at both ends left me flamed out. I was depleted by weariness and self-pity.

- Recreationally: I once adhered to a daily jogging regimen in all weathers. That actually led me to injuries, especially when running on snow and ice.

Most of the best lessons I've learned have been learned the hard way. These are the life-giving lessons that I'm seeking to share with other leaders near and far.

The lessons are all rooted in enhancing well-being versus nonstop, demanding disciplines. While I used to talk (even brag) frequently about my personal disciplines, goals, and habits, I now prefer to talk about my life-giving rhythms. Guilt may be a great short-term motivator, but only grace works well over the long term. I'm learning to focus more on the *why* and less on the *what*.

Grace-full rhythms are the key to grace-filled living. As Anne Lamott wrote, "I do not understand the mystery of grace—only that it meets us where we are and does not leave us where it found us." It all comes back to the geometry of the cross. The vertical dimension points to a love relationship with God, and the horizontal, to a love relationship with others.

By God's grace I'm making some refreshing progress on my journey of discovering life-giving, grace-full rhythms. While I'm not expecting to take up dancing in old age, I am desiring to learn more about the unforced rhythms of God's grace. How about you?

REFLECTION QUESTIONS

Has the truth of the gospel ever come crashing down on you? Describe your experience.

What's the label on your boulder?

What life rhythms are most enriching to you?

CHAPTER 6

CHOOSE PURITY

"GOD DOES NOT SAVE US FROM TEMPTATIONS. HE
SUSTAINS US IN THE MIDST OF THEM."

—OSWALD CHAMBERS

You're exceptional, and that's your problem!

The leaders I'm investing in are all exceptional:

- Exceptionally gifted
- Exceptionally resourced
- Exceptionally appreciated

And yet every gift can be abused. No one is exempt from the temptations of entitlement. Those who are exceptionally blessed can easily be deceived. Remember King Solomon. He was an exceptionally gifted man. After he humbly asked for the wisdom to lead well, the Lord stunned him with far more, saying, "I will do what you have asked. I will give you a wise and discerning heart, so that there will never be anyone like you, nor will there ever be. Moreover, I will give you what you have not asked for—both wealth and honor—so that in your lifetime you will have no equal among kings" (1 Kings 3:12–13 NIV).

Sadly, even though Solomon started well, Solomon did not finish well. Why? Well, even the wisest of the wise are still human. While Solomon saw God answer his heartfelt prayer for wisdom in ways far beyond anything he could have imagined, Solomon eventually fell into the entitlements of power. Just like his father before him, he didn't consistently use his freedom to honor God, but instead, he willfully violated the clear standards of God.

Solomon was exceptional; therefore, Solomon thought that he was the exception! That was his problem, and often ours too, and that's scary. If we're not careful, our gifting can carry us further than our character can sustain us. And the value that our society places on star quality and charisma over character doesn't help.

HAVE YOU READ THE NEWS LATELY?

In recent days we have been stunned with tragic stories of exceptionally gifted Christian leaders who crashed and burned. In their own ways, they enjoyed both exceptional gifts and exceptional freedoms, but they abused both. They brought shame to themselves, their families, and their ministries. How?

- They squandered kingdom resources.
- They committed adultery.
- They refused accountability.

No one is exempt from temptation. In a study of a hundred biblical leaders, on whom there was enough information to evaluate, it was concluded that only one-third finished well. Those who didn't finish well had the same things in common. They failed to make personal application of the Scriptures to their own lives, and they failed to exercise personal accountability with others.[31]

Without applied theology and deep community we're all sitting ducks for the devil! It's been said that unless you're stronger than Samson, more devoted than David, or wiser than Solomon, sexual sin can bring you down too!

We really don't need any more illustrations of shameful behavior among Christian leaders, but we can't escape them. A few years ago, Ravi Zacharias, an esteemed leader of international influence, famously said, "Sin will take you farther than you want to go, keep you longer than you want to stay, and cost you more than you want to pay." He also said, "Even after all these years I'm shocked at how sin still stalks me."

Well, now we know that sin didn't just "stalk" him; he actively and repeatedly pursued it! The discovery of his repeated immorality led to devastation for his family and his ministry.

The reverberations continue creating aftershocks within the Christian community to this day.

Sooner or later we will each stand before God to give an account. "For we must all appear before the judgment seat of Christ, so that each of us may receive what is due us for the things done while in the body, whether good or bad" (2 Corinthians 5:10 NIV).

Author Randy Alcorn says that the phrase "whether good or bad" in the above verse may be "the most disturbing phrase for believers in the entire New Testament."[32] Few like the sound of it; nevertheless, the Bible speaks about a coming judgment—of our works, not our sins. Our sins are covered by the sacrifice of Christ. Our rewards will be based upon our behavior.

By God's grace none of us will be defined for eternity by our worst day. Even King David's life wasn't defined that way: "For David had done what was pleasing in the LORD's sight and obeyed the LORD's commands throughout his life, except in the affair concerning Uriah the Hittite" (1 Kings 15:5).

That's the summary of David's life after his affair with Bathsheba, after he arranged the death of her husband, and after he tried to cover it all up! This means there is hope for us all, no matter how flawed, manipulative, or entitled we may at times have been!

Entitlement isn't just a problem among many millennials; it's a problem among many Christian leaders! Decades ago I read an interview with a denominational leader who said that

in his state he had never known of a pastor caught in sexual immorality who was not also guilty of financial impropriety. While
you may think of someone guilty of just one or the other, the
point is that both are based in the abuse of privilege.

YOU HAVE AN ENEMY

Seldom do we immediately see our own vulnerabilities.
Tim Keller wrote, "Self-deception is not the worst thing you can
do, but it's the means by which we do the worst things. The sin
that is most distorting your life right now is often the one you
can't see." This is why the psalmist prayed, "Keep me from lying
to myself; give me the privilege of knowing your instructions"
(Psalm 119:29).

How can we each get on track and stay on track to finish
well?

First, admit reality: you've got a relentless enemy! He will
never give up on bringing you down, so don't assume that you
will ever outgrow or age out of any temptation. A buddy of mine
recently told me of an old priest who confessed, "I wouldn't assume that I'm beyond sexual temptation until I'm in heaven for
at least three full days!" As long as you have a pulse, you'll have
some personal battles with temptation.

Finally, take heart, temptation is not sin. Jesus was tempted
in every way, and yet was without sin. Yes, He was fully Divine,
but Jesus was also fully human. Our humanity isn't the entire
problem; it's our failure to admit our humanity and take the

appropriate measures to live within God-designed limits. Living within limits is the key to godliness. We can be both human and holy.

We all must determine to do two things:

1. Faithfully devote ourselves to consistent personal application of the Bible.
2. Faithfully devote ourselves to living in honest, soul-enriching community.

These practices are essential, for the Bible says, "Who can say, 'I have cleansed my heart; I am pure and free from sin'?" (Proverbs 20:9).

(MOST) EVERYONE'S BATTLE!

The topic of temptation, particularly sexual temptation, has been described as "every man's battle." In addition, with the rapid escalation of pornography accessibility and use, it is all too often a struggle for women as well. In fact, we're now told that when it comes to porn use, where men were ten years ago, women are today! Pornography use is epidemic. While we may never have technically violated our vow of sexual fidelity, we all might admit that at points we definitely could have!

The most powerful sexual organ is the brain. We immediately get a surge of pleasure with the release of dopamine, and like any drug it can make us *dopey*! What God intended for pleasure only in the covenant of marriage is now offered immediately and free of charge via fantasy on the internet. In his insightful book *Surfing for God: Discovering the Divine Desire Beneath Sexual Struggle*, author Michael John Cusick writes,

> So how does porn go against our design as men and sabotage God's dream for us to live out our true identities? C.S. Lewis spoke to the heart of this question when he wrote about the soul damage caused by sexual fantasy (whether through masturbation or pornography) and what he called "imaginary women."

> Lewis described these "imaginary women" this way: "Always accessible, always subservient, calls for no sacrifices or adjustments, and can be endowed with erotic, and psychological attractions which no real woman can rival. Among those shadowy brides he is always adored, always the perfect lover; no demand is made . . . no mortification ever imposed on his vanity."[33]

Sex outside of the marital bond inevitably leads to bondage of the soul. What begins as a moral problem morphs into a brain problem. It's a sort of digital cocaine. For men, access to porn is like living with a bevy of naked beauties constantly beckoning you. For women, it leads to porn star standards impossible to replicate in real life. In fact, men who are regular users of porn admit that the sight of a real naked woman is to them now merely bad porn. That's one reason for the surge in use of erectile dysfunction drugs even among young men. As one young addict in Brazil told a fellow pastor friend of mine, "The devil gives with one hand but he takes with two!"

As Jesus said, "I tell you the truth, everyone who sins is a slave of sin" (John 8:34).

Sexual temptation is sly. You can be minding your own business when you're suddenly distracted. It happened to me on a speaking trip to Florida. I had just finished preaching in multiple services for a large church and was relaxing alone on the veranda of a Tampa hotel looking forward to the warm embrace of my wife that night. That's when an attractive gal suddenly showed up and sat down near me.

She wasn't subtle. It was clear that she was interested in more than mere conversation. Ironically, it happened on the seventh day of the month; therefore, I had been warned about her when reading the seventh chapter of Proverbs early that morning: "The woman approached him, seductively dressed and sly of heart" (Proverbs 7:10).

I've penciled in my Bible the names of several key kingdom leaders who have recently succumbed to sexual temptation. They're listed alongside the warnings of Proverbs 5–7 as a warning to me! As Proverbs 7:26 warns, "For she has been the ruin of many; many men have become her victims."

No Christian man or woman wants to become a "victim" or "victimizer," but all too many have. To be clear, some haven't technically been *victimized* or *fallen* into sin. At some point they willfully *stepped* into it! Perhaps it was at the gym, or at work, or even with an attractive someone they met through the church. No one is exempt from the attraction to beauty. Men are typically hardwired to appreciate the female form and to be drawn to those with attractive personalities. These sorts of attractions and temptations are not sin. It's what happens next.

AFFAIRS AREN'T ACCIDENTAL

The pattern of temptation is progressive; sometimes moving this way looks like this: appreciation –> attraction –> obsession –> degradation.

- Appreciation: acknowledging God designed beauty.
- Attraction: lingering visually on the beauty.
- Obsession: cultivating fantasies about the beauty.
- Degradation: embracing immorality with the beauty.

Immorality is always a choice, and the choice is ours. Psychologist Jay Lindsay once shared his observations about immorality first with me and then with our church in what he called the Twelve-Step Affair Process. Here's what he saw with many who had welcomed ruin into their relationships. It went this way:

1. Readiness
2. Alertness
3. Innocent Meeting
4. Intentional Meeting
5. Public Lingering
6. Private Lingering
7. Purposeful Isolating
8. Pleasurable Isolating
9. Affectionate Embracing
10. Passionate Embracing
11. Capitulation
12. Acceptance

In recent years the only change in the pattern above is in the acceleration of it. C.S. Lewis said, "No man suddenly becomes base." It's a process, and according to the experts the only difference in our culture is that the speed of the process has radically accelerated. For example, during the 2020 pandemic one porn website reported a 600 percent increase in use. Pornography is a plague bringing ruin to our culture, with 64 percent of Christian men and 15 percent of Christian women at least monthly opening the door of their hearts to the devastation of the devil. But it doesn't have to be that way!

Take heart. While sexual enticements are rooted in our humanity, sexual immorality does not have to be our destiny. Consider these truths from Scripture and take them to heart:

- "The temptations in your life are no different from what others experience. And God is faithful. He will not allow the temptation to be more than you can stand. When you are tempted, he will show you a way out so that you can endure" (1 Corinthians 10:13).
- "The Spirit who lives in you is greater than the spirit who lives in the world" (1 John 4:4).
- "For God has not given us a spirit of fear and timidity, but of power, love and self-discipline" (2 Timothy 1:7).

It's been said that all relationships are going somewhere, and that somewhere may be very good or even very bad. I once heard a sociologist say that the average man "falls in love" seven times before he gets married, and then seven more times after he gets married! If so, that's not a matter of our *destiny* but a matter of our *humanity!* Many men have confided in me that physical attraction led to an emotional connection; however, for some it was just the opposite, the emotional connection came first. Either way, for many the extra ingredient of alcohol accelerated their descent into immorality.

Temptation is always a topic in the safe setting of a covenant group. Everything mentioned briefly here is expanded on there with great soberness and soul searching. This always leads to catalytic conversations and even to humble confessions. As one pastor said, "This is holy ground . . . I don't know where else I could go to engage in a conversation like this!" Indeed, it's led to some leaders recognizing the dangerous path they were on and humbly repenting.

NOT ALL TEMPTATIONS ARE SEXUAL

Now, all temptations are not the same, and certainly not all temptations are sexual ones. In *Mere Christianity* C.S. Lewis writes,

> Though I have had to speak at some length about sex, I want to make it as clear as I possibly can that the center of Christian morality is not there. If anyone thinks that Christians regard unchastity as the supreme vice, he is quite wrong. The sins of the flesh are bad, but they are the least bad of all sins. All the worst pleasures are purely spiritual: the pleasure of putting other people in the wrong, of bossing and patronizing . . . and backbiting; the pleasure of power, of hatred. For there are two things inside me, competing with the human self which I must try to become. They are the Animal self and the Diabolical self. The Diabolical self is the worse of the two.[34]

So what is your most stubborn temptation? We're all tempted every day. Some of those temptations come from without, but most others come from within. While occasionally I may be visually tempted at the gym, it's more common for me to be tempted by the other sort—sins from within. When I'm alone in the privacy of my own home office, I face frustrations at my own desk! I can feel safe, secure, and completely calm in my study and then erupt with irritation because of some sudden interruption or another perplexing technological challenge.

What about you?

C.S. Lewis nailed me: "If there are rats in the cellar you are most likely to see them if you go in very suddenly. But the suddenness does not create the rats: it only prevents them from hiding. In the same way the suddenness of the provocation does not make me an ill-tempered man: it only shows me what an ill-tempered man I am."[35]

Just as Jesus was tempted after His baptism, so are we all! I owe a great debt to Henri Nouwen who helped me to see how the three great temptations faced by our Lord are common for us all to some degree. He shares this insight in his book *The Way of the Heart: Connecting with God Through Prayer, Wisdom, and Silence*. He calls solitude "the furnace of transformation" and says that Jesus entered into this furnace. The furnace is a purifying and testing time over what Nouwen calls "the three compulsions of the world" and he clarifies them like this:

- To be relevant ("turn stones into loaves")
- To be spectacular ("throw yourself down")
- To be powerful ("I will give you all of these kingdoms")[36]

I know which of these compulsions is currently the most tempting to me. As I read and reflect on God's Word each day, it's not hard to see the application to my own life. I crave my early morning time, and without it I would be far more vulnerable than I already am. As English Puritan Presbyterian author John Flavel has observed, "They that know God will be humble; they that know themselves cannot be proud."

Purity and humility must be my daily pursuit! This is why I repeat the same words multiple times every day: "Lord Jesus, have mercy on me!"

The choice to finish well must be made daily by each of us.

Only I can make that choice for me, and only you can make that choice for you. By God's grace, may we once again be able to say each day, "I have no secrets, and it's well with my soul."

We all hate accountability, and we're never alone. Furthermore, even if we may have formal or informal reporting systems in place, no one will be any more accountable than they want to be. We all have some private and even embarrassing things we prefer others don't ever know. For sin-prone humans, that's inevitable. However, admitting our flaws and faults doesn't disqualify us from credibility in life or even Christian leadership. It's just the opposite.

When we're more open about our failings, we end up having more influence in the lives of others. Sadly, many in leadership don't believe this. I've read somewhere that Christian leaders don't fall because they are holy, they fall because they forget they are human.

Our struggles, both recent and long ago, regularly remind us of our own humanity. I can still vividly recall a tempting situation from years ago; now that I think of it, maybe I was attracted to this gal because she looked a lot like my own wife. When she set up a counseling appointment with me, I felt my heart beat faster. So much so that it scared me. Just before she came in, I called a pastor friend and asked him to pray for me immediately and specifically! He did.

The good news is that I successfully endured that temptation. The bad news is when my pastor friend later faced a similar temptation, he didn't make a similar call, either to me or to anyone. It ended up destroying his marriage and his ministry.

THE RIGHT QUESTIONS GET TO THE HEART OF THE MATTER

If you were struggling with temptation—thinking about having an affair or merely imagining such a thing—who would you tell? Not one of us is as strong as we wish we were. We all need those who will partner with us in pursuing soul strength.

For this reason, several decades ago, psychologist Dr. John Walker, a close friend, and I began talking weekly and meeting regularly. Each time, we asked each other five F.A.C.E.T. questions that addressed what we were Focusing on, Accepting, Choosing, Enjoying, and Trusting. We then customized the questions to reflect what each of us was prioritizing in that season of our lives.

Here are the questions that I invited John to ask me each week:

- Are you Focusing on your wife or fantasizing about other women?
- Are you Accepting the limitations of others without becoming critical or frustrated?
- Are you Choosing what you want and need to do, or are you obsessing over shoulds?
- Are you Enjoying a sabbath and having fun?
- Are you Trusting that God knows your name? (Isaiah 43:1)

My close friends know my insecurities well. That's why John regularly emphasized that God's grace wasn't just for others . . . it was for me! I need that. I need to be reminded that God is with me, God is for me, and that others are as well. I don't want or need "accountability" as much as I want and need acceptance and encouragement. How about you? For most of us, asking for accountability almost sounds like inviting someone to snoop around in our dirty laundry.

I don't want to hold others accountable; I want to hold them close.

Inviting others to ask you questions that encourage authenticity and deep conversation is a wonderful tool. Customized F.A.C.E.T. questions are one example.

At times we also customize other "tough love" questions as well. None are asked with a spirit of condemnation, but out of compassion and concern. It's amazing how open men will be when they feel understood, accepted, and encouraged. In fact, the more we share our struggles, the more we grow to trust that we're not alone. We really feel like brothers.

Other questions that encourage authenticity and deep conversation include what I call "the 4 Ds." I created these years ago and continue to use them as a conversational template in group gatherings, and even with close friends with whom I long to go deeper. get-togethers with close friends with whom I long to go deeper.

The four Ds stand for Delight, Drain, Discovery, Determination. Here are the questions:

Delight: What is *sparking joy* for you? This could be anything from a new puppy to a new baby, a gratifying hobby or a happy activity. *So, what's been uplifting to you?*

Drain: What's *disturbing* you? This could be anything that's personally depleting, i.e. the Covid chaos or a personal conflict, a lack of sleep or the lies you keep telling yourself. *So, what's recently been disheartening to you?*

Discovery: What's *enlightening* you? This could be something that has seized you through your Bible reading or that is ennobling you through your other learnings. *So, what's been especially illuminating and encouraging to you?*

Determination: What's *inspiring you*? This could be a new exercise or eating regimen, an upcoming getaway or adventure. We're all driven by new dreams. *So, what's ahead that's invigorating and exciting to you?*

These four questions are gold! They have been powerful for us, for our families, and for all the groups that we lead and facilitate. They work over lunch tables, in small groups, among business leaders, even on the mission field. Twenty pastors serving in the slums of Nairobi are now using them to build healthy relationships with the people they lead.

I've been using these questions with a group of business guys I'm mentoring in applied theology. In preparing to personally unpack their 4 D's with the group each week, I encourage them to journal their insights. One of the men, Jamison, is co-owner of a small tech business.

Jamison says, "Because my brain runs faster than my fingers, I've always hated slowing down to write things down. Now I'm discovering through journaling with a pen and paper that I'm calmer than ever."

Along with the rest of us, he's discovering that pausing to ponder on paper is highly productive. God speaks most clearly when we get quiet for the sake of our soul. But someone has to take the lead, both in introducing them and in answering them.

In our soul care covenant group model, these questions are vital. They are part of the rhythm of every gathering and conversation we have, and it has yet to get stale. Just the opposite. This template catalyzes deeper reflection and conversation. The 4 Ds are life-giving for us and for all we've been privileged to share them with.

REFLECTION QUESTIONS

Which of the three temptations Jesus faced—to be relevant, spectacular, or powerful—is the most alluring to you?

Have you ever been shocked by a temptation?

What question do you need someone to ask you?

CHAPTER 7

LIVE GENEROUSLY

"I HAVE NEVER MET AN UNHAPPY GENEROUS
PERSON."

—TODD HARPER

Life is a never-ending series of unexpected happenings and life-clarifying experiences that could happen at any time. No one really knows what's going to happen next; that's why we're called to live by faith, not by sight.

Several years ago, our neighborhood was shocked by a brazen burglary. When a family near us was vacationing in Italy, their beautiful home was burglarized. To make matters worse, it happened repeatedly over several days. In broad daylight. What's really amazing is that the break-ins were not discovered until most everything of value had been taken out of the house. As our friends later told us, "The thieves took half of our things—and it was the good half!"

How would you feel if you lost half of your stuff—and it was the good half? Truth be told, most of us could get along quite well with only half of the stuff we possess. But that still doesn't keep us from adding to our stuff. The average home is not only three times larger than the homes when I was growing up, but the average home has literally thousands of items. That's true for most all of us even though we know that the most important things in life aren't things at all.

Our youngest daughter and her husband have proven that. They recently moved out of a 3,700-square-foot home filled with stuff and hit the road in a thirty-seven-foot RV. They and their two little boys are now starting the second year of a nomadic adventure and loving every day of it. They've learned that living lighter isn't just possible, but in many ways it is preferable. They're enjoying life far more as they are living with far less. They've traded more stuff for more stories!

And they're not alone!

Studies show that many people report how their happiness is linked to simplicity and generosity. In fact, it's been documented that self-esteem goes up as giving goes up!

BE GENEROUS, FOR GOD'S SAKE!

Now, let's face it, Jesus wasn't first concerned about our positive self-image but about calling us to a positive purpose. That purpose is to honor God by partnering with God—we are never more like God than when we give. Jesus made that clear

in one of the most famous accounts of his ministry recorded in
Luke 21:1–4 (NIV):

> As Jesus looked up, he saw the rich putting their gifts
> into the temple treasury. He also saw a poor widow put
> in two very small copper coins. "Truly I tell you," he
> said, "this poor widow has put in more than all the oth-
> ers. All these people gave their gifts out of their wealth;
> but she out of her poverty put in all she had to live on."

As Pastor Greg Surratt, of Seacoast Community Church,
noted in a sermon, Jesus is taking notes on your generosity.

Question: do you keep good notes on your own generosity? Do you keep good financial records? We do; in fact, we've
saved the records of every expenditure since we were married in
August 1968. In many ways it's not only a record of our life but
of our priorities. Guess what? It's not only financially wise but
biblically based to do this! "Be sure you know the condition of
your flocks, give careful attention to your herds; for riches do
not endure forever" (Proverbs 27:23–24 NIV).

When our kids were growing up, our budget was tight so
we taught them the 10/10/80 plan. That's give at least 10 percent, save at least 10 percent, and carefully manage the rest. That
pattern has served our family and church family very well over
the years.

Now, as with most of you, we love to give to Christ-hon-
oring work, especially through our local church. Mark Moore,

acclaimed author and teaching pastor at Christ's Church of the Valley in Phoenix, Arizona, said, "When we give through the church we make Jesus famous. When we give as individuals we make ourselves famous."

I want to make Jesus famous, don't you? I want people to come to Jesus, and therefore, most of what we give is through the church of Jesus and to other Christian causes through the National Christian Foundation. Giving through honorable nonprofit organizations is good stewardship.

Having our charitable giving twice audited by the IRS, we've learned just how important it is to keep good records. However, that means that someone at the church or NCF also has to keep those records. If we're going to make a tax-deductible gift, someone has to know what we gave and be able to verify it.

But wait—didn't Jesus warn us not to give so that others would see us? Yes He did; that's in Matthew 6:3–4 (NIV): "But when you give to the needy, do not let your left hand know what your right hand is doing, so that your giving may be in secret. Then your Father, who sees what is done in secret, will reward you."

Clearly both the *motive* and the *manner* of what we give are noted in heaven so that we will receive a heavenly blessing. However, Jesus didn't say we forfeit a blessing if someone *might* find out what we give. He is clearly warning that we may forfeit the blessing if we give *so that* others will find out. That would be giving to make ourselves famous and not Jesus. Our motive matters.

What might the "blessing" of giving be? I suspect that it will be the fulfillment of realizing all the eternal good that was accomplished through what we gave while on Earth. When we get to heaven, we will be privileged to see things as they truly are and to celebrate that we partnered with God in ushering others into His eternal embrace. That's why the greatest portion of our giving should be directed to efforts that bring people to Christ and help the desperately poor. That's typically the local church.

Note that the poor widow brought her offering to the temple. This was the central place of worship for the Jewish people. The bringing of their firstfruits, a tithe or 10 percent of everything they received, was considered to be a worship requirement. However, for the Jews, giving didn't stop at 10 percent. They also gave offerings beyond that, and some say those offerings totaled about 23 percent. Therefore, some argue that we really aren't giving until we've exceeded the level of 10 percent of our income. I have long held that view myself, and I know the same is true for many pastors.

GENEROSITY HAS MANY LEVELS

Tithing is the beginning of our stewardship, not the ending. Randy Alcorn has said, "God prospers me not to raise my standard of living but to raise my standard of giving."

As I see it, there are really three levels of giving:

- The Devotion Level—Faithfulness in returning the first 10 percent. A tithe is a great place to start but a lousy place to stop.

- The Inspiration Level—Generosity prompted by special needs or opportunities. We always need to be open to promptings to share.
- The Revelation Level—Responding to a clear call of God with radical, even life-altering generosity. Something far beyond the reasonable.

My wife and I know some who have given everything away. Others with modest incomes have chosen to give at least half of their incomes every year. Generosity stories have always served to inspire us all. As the psalmist describes those who fear the Lord, "They share freely and give generously to those in need. Their good deeds will be remembered forever. They will have influence and honor" (Psalm 112:9).

What I penciled in my Bible is this: "Joyful generosity is the finest legacy."

I once enjoyed a memorable conversation on an airplane. I had just met the man seated near me the night before at a leadership meeting. We were both surprised to discover we were traveling on the same flight and seated in the same row with an open seat between us. I rarely talk much at all on a plane, much less have an actual conversation. This is one I'll never forget. As the flight progressed, so did our personal connection as we began to talk about the things that mattered most to each of us. That's when Jack made a statement unlike any I had ever heard from anyone else before: "Alan, I just want to be remembered as a generous man!"

How do you want to be remembered? On the last day it won't matter what sort of house we lived in or car we drove or the size of our flat screen TV. The only thing that will matter is what we did *with* Jesus and what we did *for* Jesus. Rather than living with a scarcity mentality, we ought to live with a generosity mentality. God blesses us all to be a blessing. Many times that's with our treasures, but the same principle also applies to our time and talents. As I've heard it said, "You don't have to feed the five thousand. You just have to bring your loaves and fishes."

My passion is to live generously, seeking more *for* others than *from* others. As Pete Ochs, a faith-based entrepreneur and author, has said, it's about a stewardship of all of life: our labor, our influence, our finances, and our expertise. Finances are just one dimension of living generously. When it comes to money, many people have a spending strategy. Some have an investment strategy. Few have a giving strategy.

GOD CARES ABOUT GENEROSITY

Even though God's Word is clear on the topic of money, most of God's people ignore it. Far fewer than 10 percent of Christians even give the base biblical amount of 10 percent. After I taught on this topic for many years, my pastor friends took notice. One of them reached out to me suggesting that we coauthor a small book together on the topic. In fact, he asked me on two separate occasions. Each time I didn't feel the time was right.

Fast-forward a few years and I learned that same pastor was fired. The reason? Even though he was overseeing the staff of a large church, it was discovered that he had not been tithing himself. Not even close. Then after repeated warnings he was released due to his lack of moral authority, and rightly so. Richard Halverson, esteemed U.S. minister and author, has said, "Money is an exact index to a man's true character."

I can't imagine the embarrassment of getting caught as *ungenerous*!

Then again, being ungenerous is not all that unusual even for some in leadership. A couple once visited our church and heard their first message on tithing. They had just come from a small congregation where the husband had been one of the leaders. While driving home after the message, he told his wife, "Wow, I've never heard anything like that! Last year we gave a total of just three hundred dollars. We've got to fix that!"

Fix it they did! They immediately began to tithe and rapidly moved far beyond that. They didn't give to get rich, but God definitely soon made them rich. He surprised them, and still does, with uncommon resources to steward, and it is one of the great joys of their lives. Recently they said, "The best decision of our life was coming to Rocky Mountain Christian Church. The tithing message changed everything!"

OUR RESPONSE TO MONEY BECOMES OUR TESTIMONY

Money in the hands of a generous person is a force multiplier. It's both a test and a trust. What we do with it becomes a testimony. Making money to make a difference is a noble thing. Lavish giving, not lavish living, is God's standard for His people. As one single mother in our congregation said, "I love tithing because it makes me feel so rich!"

My parents faithfully modeled tithing and generosity for me. One of my early memories was putting a dime of every dollar I earned in my offering envelope every Sunday. I remember sitting in church anticipating the offering and thinking, *Whoever opens this envelope may think my dime is no big deal. But it's my tithe of my dollar. I want to do this because I want to be faithful to God and to His church!*

When I was a kid, finances were always tight for our family. On one occasion we were basically down to ketchup in the pantry. Our mother gathered my sisters and me in the kitchen, and as we held hands, she humbly prayed for provision.

Shortly after that my mother entered a design contest. The challenge was to remodel an entire kitchen for maximum efficiency and to submit a design using the maximum number of the company's kitchen cabinets and appliances. She won! We still didn't have an abundance of food in the house, but we sure did have a beautiful new kitchen to prepare it in!

God has an unlimited capacity to bless anyone. During one of the worst financial crises our church ever faced, an impressive young visitor surprised me. Harmony introduced herself and humbly said, "I saw something and felt you should hear this. You need to have your hands open for wisdom to steward the resources God is going to send you."

Her words and humble demeanor made an unforgettable impact on me. That was many years ago, and I continue to live with the confidence that God can surprise me at any time! As 2 Chronicles 16:9 (NASB) reminds us, "For the eyes of the LORD roam throughout the earth, so that He may strongly support those whose heart is completely His."

Who doesn't want God's strong support? Every family of faith desires God's blessing, but too many are not yet ready to receive His blessing.

Some years ago the church I led instituted what we called a 90-Day Tithing Challenge with a money-back guarantee. We promised to give a full refund to anyone who began to tithe and failed to experience God's blessing. We let each one define what "blessing" meant. Guess what? After many hundreds of people took up the 90-day challenge, only two ever asked for their money back.

One was a single parent who gave no explanation but still received a full refund. The other was the husband of a woman with severe medical needs. He came to the elders explaining his predicament and the need to pay for expensive prescription medications. The elders wisely encouraged him to continue tithing but promised to cover the entire cost of the needed medications from the benevolence budget of the church. Once again, godly leaders gave wise and godly advice.

WHAT WILL YOUR STORY BE?

Have you yet responded to the bold advice to trust God and tithe? The reality is that at some point we all have managed to survive on at least 10 percent less than we do now. In truth, most of us are far richer than we ever expected to be. I just wish my parents had known that they never needed to live with financial angst. God was always their personal financial advisor, and true to His Word, He always excessively provided in His time. What do you wish your parents had known about money? What do you wish your parents had taught you about money?

Wealth is having everything you need to do everything God wants you to do. On a mission trip to Brazil I was invited to the home of an unemployed laborer. It was a simple house for a family of four, but they were honored to welcome me. After a brief visit I was invited to the kitchen to enjoy chocolate cake. I made a joke that it must be someone's birthday.

The woman responded by saying, "No, we can't afford cake for birthdays. We only have cake for special occasions."

I was beyond humbled because I was the definition of a special occasion!

Have you ever been humbled by generosity? I've had that happen too many times to count. One of the most memorable times was in our first experience with a Journey of Generosity retreat. We watched a video featuring the story of an employee at a Great Harvest Bakery.

Kathryn had been saving money to replace her car. But when she learned of a friend in greater need, she gave her entire savings to help. All $5,000 of it!

When the story of Kathryn's radical generosity leaked out, several stepped in. They didn't merely replenish her empty car account, they bought her a car. A new car! You will have to watch the story to get the full impact. I've now seen it a half dozen times and it never fails to inspire me (to watch the video, go to https://youtu.be/LIASx_kTv8M).

Whenever I feel a little too proud of my own giving level compared with others, I think of people like Kathryn. We have now led a number of these generosity events, and each one reminds me of what Bryan Chrisman told me years ago. Bryan is a leader with the National Christian Foundation, so I knew I could get some good wisdom from him. When I was grappling with how much is enough to give, Bryan told me, "In the journey of generosity, someone will always be ahead of us and others behind."

Leaders in generosity inspire me! Eric Most is another leader with NCF. He once said, "We don't merely give for the tax savings but for the spreading of multiple levels of joy."

GENEROUS PEOPLE ARE JOYFUL PEOPLE

Joy is the goal. Whenever my wife, Linda, and I have dipped our toes in the deepest waters of generous giving, we have also experienced the deepest joy. But that hasn't always been easy. C.S. Lewis wrote in *Mere Christianity*, "I do not believe one can settle how much we ought to give. I am afraid the only safe rule is to give more than we can spare. In other words, if our expenditure on comforts, luxuries, amusements, etc., is up to the standard common among those with the same income as our own, we are probably giving away too little."[37]

We've all heard it said that you can't outgive God. Have you ever discovered the reality of that? After hosting and funding a Journey of Generosity retreat for six couples, we saw again that the joy of giving is contagious. Our desire to be generous was spiked by our friends.

When we returned home, I read an insight from pastor and author Chip Ingram: "Generosity is a gateway to intimacy with God." That's true; however, what hit me was that generosity had done something else for us as well. Our decision to host a retreat also served as a gateway to intimacy with others! We'll never forget what God did that weekend. The "return on our investment" once again far exceeded our expectations!

Sometimes the price we pay to bless others generously is priceless for them. I am privileged to serve now on the National Christian Foundation's advisory council as a "champion of generosity." If you'd like more information on experiences like we've had or the library of resources of the NCF, go to ncfgiving.com/ givingstrategy.

This I know: money matters to everyone! That's why in some form or fashion it comes up over two thousand times in the Bible! In the book *Money Matters: Faith, Life, and Wealth,* the authors say, "Money grabs at the heart. It is not neutral. It is a power. It can be a radioactive issue. We want to have money, but money wants to have us."[38]

Remember the neighbors I referenced at the beginning of this chapter who had half of their stuff stolen—the good half? I talked with them when they returned from their Italian vacation and was surprised how unaffected they were by the burglary.

That's when Brian and Andrea said, "Well, the timing of the burglary was amazing. Not just because we were in Italy at the time, but because we had just toured the Village of Assisi where St. Francis had lived centuries ago. Francis had been born into the home of a wealthy merchant but gave it all up to serve the poor."

That's when they received the call about the burglary and the report that half of their stuff had been taken, but they were completely unshaken. Why? They immediately realized that the most important things in life aren't things at all.

What would it take for you to move beyond what many call the tyranny of things? Hopefully it won't be a burglary or a deathbed discovery.

As Andy Stanley has said, "Do you want more stuff or do you want more stories?" This is a vital question and a vital topic when it comes to strength of soul.

It's impossible to have a strong soul if you have a stingy heart!

REFLECTION QUESTIONS

Have you ever lived with financial fear?

When have you been surprised by God's generosity to you through others?

How have the most generous people you know inspired you?

CHAPTER 8

ACCEPT YOUR LIMITS

"WE WILL NOT BOAST ABOUT THINGS DONE
OUTSIDE OUR AREA OF AUTHORITY. WE WILL BOAST
ONLY ABOUT WHAT HAS HAPPENED WITHIN THE
BOUNDARIES OF THE WORK GOD HAS GIVEN US,
WHICH INCLUDES OUR WORKING WITH YOU."

—2 CORINTHIANS 10:13

News flash: you can't do anything and everything you want to do! Every life is a limited life. Limited by ability, capacity, and opportunity. That's by the plan of God.

I was pondering the theme of limits as I was swimming laps, repeatedly reminding myself to stay in my lane. Whenever I get out of my lane, it's not good for anyone.

I'm regularly reminded that boundaries are good for my soul as well. Certainly everything that needs to be done doesn't need to be done right now or by me. Early in my ministry I was intrigued by the thought of limited responsibility—even for Jesus. Jesus prayed to His Father, "I brought you glory to you here on earth by completing the work you gave me to do" (John 17:4).

At first I wondered how Jesus could say that. After all he obviously hadn't fed all the hungry, healed all the sick, raised all the dead, or taught all the people. Then it dawned on me. The special assignment given even to Jesus was less than the total need! The same is true for us all. No one is called to do everything.

Too often I'm pushing the limits of life. Even now I often must discipline myself not to work (or write) late into the night. For years I confused the flow of adrenaline with the flow of the Spirit. I came to realize that just because I was in my high-energy mode, it didn't mean others were excited to join me.

I'll never forget leading a staff retreat years ago when I discovered this. We had just finished a late feast at a busy restaurant. I was expecting to return immediately to lead yet another session. I soon learned that I was the only one assuming that. Everyone else was assuming that we'd had enough heady stuff for the day. Instead, what we most needed was to take a break and enjoy the heart stuff of simply relaxing together. As they all laughed at my lack of awareness, I got the point. Slowly.

Chalk that up as one of my blind spots. It's easy for me to speed up and lose out on the moment.

DO YOU KNOW WHAT THE WORD *SABBATH* REALLY MEANS?

When it comes to exceeding life's speed limits, I'm not alone. This is why the Lord instituted the Sabbath rhythm. The word literally means "to stop"!

God's people were told not just to take a break but to set aside one day a week for worship, rest, and renewal of the soul. Samuel Chadwick, a Wesleyan Methodist leader of the last century, has said that hurry is the death of prayer. We might also say that hurry is the death of depth and a healthy, thriving soul!

There's a story of a visitor to Africa who learned this from the porters carrying his belongings. After several days of travel, one morning the porters didn't leave camp. The visitor asked what the delay was all about. He was told the wise natives were waiting for their souls to catch up with their bodies!

Sabbath is intended to be a life-enriching gift of God to us all. In the revised edition of her classic book *Soul Feast,* Marjorie Thompson includes a chapter called "Reclaiming Sabbath Time: The Sacred Art of Ceasing." She says, "Valuing and guarding the sacred rhythm of sabbath is a radical choice, particularly in a culture as devoted as ours to production and achievement."[39]

She began the chapter recalling when a friend made reference to "the beauty of the borders." Author Flora Wuellner reminded everyone that landscapes are made more beautiful by fences, hedges, and flowerbeds. It's certainly true in our yard.

Several years ago we added tons of rock, mulch, and fresh edging to better define the landscape. As a result, there's hardly a day that goes by I don't enjoy a visual feast.

There's definite value in clear definition of our landscapes and our lives. One of my new weekly sabbath rhythms is simply to review the prior week with the 4 Ds of delight, drain, discovery, and determination. I began to do this in preparation for leading a small soul care circle of men at church as a way to bring them into my world. I didn't expect this ten-minute rhythm to help reacquaint me with my own!

Now, as every week passes, I look back and view it as remarkable!

WHEN AND WHERE DO YOU PONDER?

There is great value in pondering. The same goes for another more extensive practice called R.A.P.: Review-Analysis-Plan. I used to do this monthly for my intercessors; now I do it quarterly. Frankly, it's a chore to start, but it's one that consistently leads to soul-gratifying discovery. Here's what the Bible says about each step of this practice.

- Review: "I pondered the direction of my life, and I turned to follow your laws" (Psalm 119:59).
- Analysis: "Speak, Lord, your servant is listening" (1 Samuel 3:9).
- Plan: "If you plan to do good, you will receive unfailing love and faithfulness" (Proverbs 14:22).

I use a simple bullet outline to take note of the highlights in each category. Then I write a few paragraphs of analysis. Finally I add a few more bullets to identify upcoming opportunities I'm intending to pursue.

My paper calendar is my friend. I use a digital calendar only for a few things. I use a paper calendar for most things. I ponder better on paper. Some call it the new technology.

Our leadership culture is long on performance metrics but short on pondering. This I know: my reflectiveness is key to my effectiveness. The more time I invest in reflection, the more effective my life investments seem to be. This is part of my daily, weekly, monthly, and annual soul-enriching rhythm.

I began to learn this lesson as a young boy when bored in church. Even though the messages were brilliantly presented, much of it went over my head. As my friends could attest, I had a serious "drug problem": I was *drug* to church by my parents for Sunday school and worship every week, then *drugged* again every Sunday night for youth group and yet another sermon. Even though I often found little to hold my attention, I still remember the value of stopping and sitting still. In fact, I came to refer to Sunday as "my thinking day."

When is your thinking day? Where is your thinking place? Ward Beecher, another famous American clergyman as well as activist, once said, "Wherever you have seen God pass, mark it, and go and sit in that window again."

Here's yet another insightful word from Oswald Chambers that refreshed me this very morning:

> We must have a specially selected place for prayer, but once we get there this plague of wandering thoughts begins, as we begin to think to ourselves, "This needs to be done, and I have to do that today." Jesus says to "Shut your door." Having a secret stillness before God means deliberately shutting the door on our emotions and remembering Him. God is in secret, and He sees us from "the secret place," — He does not see us as other people do, or as we see ourselves . . . Unless you learn to open the door of your life completely and let God in from your first waking moment of each new day, you will be working on the wrong level throughout the day. But if you will swing the door of your life fully open and "pray to your Father who is in the secret place," every public thing in your life will be marked with the lasting imprint of the presence of God.

My "secret place" is my home study with a beautiful picture window looking out on a small park. It's the place where I cultivate contemplation on a daily basis. In addition, I've placed two important reminders for myself on a chair in the corner. The first was a surprise from my mother. She did a needlepoint from a scribbled note I wrote when I was eight years old. Evidently, I hung the warning on my bedroom door to keep my sisters away: "This is my room where I kin go and no buddy kin hurt me."

We're all in need of a safe place. Where do you go where no one can hurt you?

What are the reminders there that help you to remember your little part in God's grand purpose?

WHAT WILL GOD SAY TO YOU?

The second reminder on my kneeling chair is a simple plaque that reads "Be still, and know that I am God" (Psalm 46:10).

Not that long ago I was having difficulty getting my wife to see the wisdom of my side of an argument. Suddenly I thought of yet another illustration that would surely seal the deal and convince her how right I was.

Just before I joined her for lunch, I began to kneel, and when I did I was arrested by the reminder of Psalm 46:10: "Be still, and know that I am God." I couldn't help but chuckle. I prayed, "Okay, I get it! I need to shut up and say no more and let You convince her!"

I don't recall the debate, but I do recall that we actually enjoyed a tension-free lunch. Then again, maybe that was the answer to my prayer. As Solomon said, "A truly wise person uses few words; a person with understanding is even-tempered" (Proverbs 17:27).

I'm slowly learning the value of an unspoken thought! As one wise man put it, "The difference between a bad marriage and a good marriage is leaving about three things unsaid every day." This is vital wisdom for me. My strength is using words. My weakness is using too many words! Time and again I've had to learn the important lesson of saying less, not more.

John Ortberg has written a helpful book entitled *Soul Keeping: Caring for the Most Important Part of You.* He shares the story of when Dr. Dallas Willard, esteemed professor of philosophy at USC, was being challenged by an arrogant student. Instead of correcting him, he simply and gently closed the class. Later he was asked why he didn't correct and demolish his young critic. Dallas replied, "I was practicing the discipline of not having the last word."[40] That's powerful!

When our church was in a protracted and expensive land use battle with Boulder County, we needed help. We enlisted the counsel of the leading land use attorneys in the state. Attorneys Darrell Waas and Kathryn Hopping were invaluable.

In preparation for my testimony in federal court, Kathryn coached me about not saying too much. She also coached me not to answer questions no one was asking and definitely not to try to be funny. I had to work at them all, especially the last one. When the time came for my lengthy testimony in court, it went very well but not as well as I wanted.

In the private debrief with Kathryn she knew how frustrated I was. I was thoroughly bummed by not having more time to communicate our case clearly and passionately. It didn't take long for Kathryn to sober me by saying, "Alan, it doesn't all depend upon you! We've got a strong case and a strong roster of witnesses. Relax, it doesn't all depend on you!" That's why I often called her Kathryn the Great!

Learning to relax in the sovereignty of God is a lifelong challenge for many. In his book *You Gotta Keep Dancin'*, Tim Hansel tells how he had to learn this lesson after a serious back injury while mountain climbing. A friend sent him a plaque with the words "Tim, Trust me. I have everything under control! Jesus."[41]

Ironically, the glass on the plaque was broken during shipping. Tim said he never had it replaced. He considered the message to be even more powerful behind shattered glass.

How is it that some seem to hear God speak so profoundly and others don't? For me the key is quiet. Here's the secret: God rarely shouts; He mostly whispers.

We're told in Psalm 25:14 (NIV), "The LORD confides in those who fear him." In Proverbs 3:32 (NIV) we read that the Lord "takes the upright into his confidence." In other words, "He is intimate with the upright" (Proverbs 3:32 NASB). Intimacy means pressed closely together for the purpose of confidential communication. Dallas Willard says, "People are meant to live in an on-going conversation with God, speaking and being spoken to by Him."

BOUNDARIES WE CHOOSE FOR OURSELVES

God seems to speak to me mostly about my attitude. He reminds me daily to shift my focus from my problems to His presence and His promise of provision. I know I'm not alone in that.

As Proverbs 15:15 (NIV) tells us, "All the days of the oppressed are wretched, but the cheerful heart has a continual feast." And Proverbs 15:30 says, "A cheerful look brings joy to the heart; good news makes for good health."

On one of our trips to Africa we met a little girl in need of a sponsor. Ivine lives with her family in the Mathare Valley slum in Nairobi. After several years of correspondence, she shared her favorite passage from the Bible with us.

"I will praise you, Lord, with all my heart; I will tell of all the marvelous things you have done. I will be filled with joy because of you. I will sing praises to your name, O Most High" (Psalm 9:1-2).

Ivine radiates an irrepressible joy even though she lives with her family of twelve in a small shanty. They have a tiny house with no windows, light or plumbing. Yet this passage focusing on praising the Lord is her favorite, proving once again that joy is just a choice away. That's true even in what many call "the slum of the slums" of Nairobi!

Could it be that we can all choose cheerfulness? By personality type some people seem predisposed to see more of the dreariness of life, while others seem predisposed to see more of the delightfulness. However, I believe that ultimately it is our choice that determines our degree of cheerfulness.

We don't have to live in perpetual dismay; in fact, the Lord clearly tells us not to! "So do not fear, for I am with you; do not be dismayed, for I am your God. I will strengthen you and help you; I will uphold you with my righteous right hand" (Isaiah 41:10 NIV).

The leaders I mentor are facing tough times right now, the toughest in our leadership lifetime! If anyone ever needs more documentation of bad news, I've always got some. Not a day goes by that I'm not deeply disturbed, not only by national news but even more by some of the behind-the-scenes reports I hear from church leaders near and far.

These are hard times. But whenever I overdose on despairing media messages, God's Word helps me to reframe everything. Life is a nonstop litany of hard hits and heart hits, but Jesus said, "Take heart! I have overcome the world" (John 16:33 NIV).

Now, when I quickly review the local, national, and world news, I already know it's going to be bad news. That's why I try to approach the news with a determined cheerfulness. First, I seek to severely limit my exposure to the bad news of the day. Then, when I do briefly read or review it, I do so against the banner of my Lord's call to take heart, for He has overcome the world! As the editors of *World Magazine* regularly remind us, "No matter the news, the purpose of the Lord prevails." Pastor Chuck Swindol sums it up well: "God is not sometimes sovereign."

No one escapes hard times. I once was embarrassed after sharing some of my laments and complaints only to learn that the man I was talking with had been riddled with a series of tragedies far beyond anything I had endured. When I apologized for my whining, he surprised me by saying, "That's okay, everyone has their own definition of hard." I was humbled by his grace.

When a good friend struggled with his wife's early-onset Alzheimer's, his long good-bye began. It was heartbreaking for Walt and his children. When I asked how he endured this great grief, he said that he was learning the power of Isaiah 61:3. He was choosing to put on a garment of praise for the spirit of heaviness.

Life is hard for everyone, but God is good! That's why the psalmist said, "Why, my soul, are you downcast? Why so disturbed within me? Put your hope in God, for I will yet praise him, my Savior and my God" (Psalm 42:5 NIV). That refrain is repeated three times in Psalm 42 and 43 as we see David telling himself to cheer up!

In *New Morning Mercies*, Paul David Tripp sharpened this reality for me. He writes, "No one is more influential in your life than you are because no one talks to you more than you do. It's a fact that you and I are in an endless conversation with ourselves. Most of us have learned that it's best not to move our lips because people will think we're crazy, but we never stop talking to ourselves."[42]

What have you been saying to yourself lately? Dr. David Martyn Lloyd-Jones, a physician turned pastor, said, "The central cause of spiritual depression is due to the fact that you are listening to yourself instead of talking to yourself!"[43]

I, for one, need to talk to myself every day, all day. Again, my friend Dr. Wes Beavis reminds us that part of our pain is always under our control. "When you experience pain, the story that you tell yourself about the experience can exacerbate or reduce the pain. You get to write the story."

The message I repeatedly need to write and to hear is clear:

- *Cheer up—there is One who redeems all things!*
- *Cheer up—the position of Savior has been taken!*
- *Cheer up—now is not forever!*
- *Cheer up—the purpose of the Lord will prevail!*
- *Cheer up—by God's grace the best is yet to be!*
- *Cheer up—Jesus has overcome the world!*

WISE FRIENDS SPEAK THE TRUTH IN LOVE

One of the marks of maturity is to listen well to those who are wiser. How long has it been since someone gave you the gift of their insight?

During a recent covenant group video call it was obvious that a heavy cloud hung over the heads of several. That's when I repeated a line I've often shared with those stuck in the mud of difficulty. I said in prayer, "Lord, for those a little low on hope right now, help them to borrow some of mine, since you've given me some extra to spare."

A few minutes later one of the guys asked me to repeat what he heard me pray.

What are the things that you need regularly repeated for you? Even if we are not slow learners, we tend to be quick forgetters! We need to be reminded time and again of God's faithfulness. We are not alone, we have not been forgotten, we are not without hope. He is here.

It's been said, "It ain't what we know that hurts us. It's what we know that ain't so." In his enlightening book *The Body Keeps the Score*, Dr. Bessel van der Kolk shares a profound insight from his mentor, psychiatrist Dr. Elvin Semrad: "The greatest sources of our suffering are the lies we tell ourselves."[44]

After listening to a leader share his self doubts and fears, I sometimes surprise him with a rebuke. "You're a big stinkin' liar! Stop lying to yourself! You're neither helpless nor hopeless. Christ is in you and He is for you!"

That's not a put-down but a call-up! Proverbs 27:6 (NIV) reminds us, "Wounds from a friend can be trusted." We all need a few who are intentionally intrusive—who have the freedom to correct and challenge us and stop us from saying soul-depleting stupid stuff to ourselves or about ourselves.

Sheriff Joe Pelle is one of my oldest friends. We've been close since long before his five consecutive terms as the sheriff of

Boulder County. We've met monthly for decades to encourage one another. One day over lunch I shared a simple set of questions I was prompted by that morning from Proverbs 15. Joe liked them so much, he went on to share them with his senior staff.

- What wise advice have you recently received? "The lips of the wise give good advice" (Proverbs 15:7).

- Who are your wise advisers? "Plans go wrong for lack of advice; many advisers bring success" (Proverbs 15:22).

- What constructive criticism have you recently listened to? "If you listen to constructive criticism, you will be at home among the wise" (Proverbs 15:31).

Every one of us has a few blind spots; unfortunately, we don't know what they are. If we did, they wouldn't be blind spots! If we already knew everything everyone else knew, we wouldn't need to ask others to share their insights, much less listen to them.

I frequently refer to my wife as my most loyal critic and my wisest counselor. After dinner with another ministry couple, I kindly challenged the husband to set his adamancy aside and listen more to his wife. My friend bristled a bit and quickly challenged me. He pointedly asked Linda, "So when has Alan recently listened to your rebuke?"

She didn't even take a breath before responding, "That actually just happened. He was preparing to head to the gym for yet another indoor cycling class on a beautiful day. He sometimes gets stuck in his routines, so I said, 'Instead of doing aerobic activity indoors on a sunny day and listening to an instructor yelling at you to keep going faster, while you're going nowhere, why don't you go swimming at the beautiful outdoor pool in town?' He reluctantly agreed, and so I told him what to do. I even packed his bag with everything he needed like he was a little kid. But he did it! Now, it's his new favorite exercise!"

Who knows you well enough to speak the truth in love to you?

My closest friends definitely take turns speaking the truth in love to me. Often it's deeply encouraging. I will always treasure the words of Cam Huxford when I was reeling from overlapping crises. I was so emotionally exhausted that I wasn't appreciating God's sustaining grace. That's when Cam said, "You encountered 'the perfect storm' but still got the ship safely back to port. In Savannah we say, 'you can prepare for a storm but you can't prepare for a hurricane—you can only pray to survive!'"

I later found this in Psalm 107:29–32:

He calmed the storm to a whisper
    and stilled the waves.
What a blessing was that stillness
    as he brought them safely into harbor!

Let them praise the LORD for his great love
  and for the wonderful things he has done for them.
Let them exalt him publicly before the congregation
  and before the leaders of the nation.

Crises are inevitable in leadership. It's not if but when and to what degree they hit us all. Everyone needs a safe person to process the hits and hurts of life in leadership.

BOUNDARIES MAKE GOOD WORKS SUSTAINABLE

Many in law enforcement understand this. In my monthly conversations my friend, Boulder County Sheriff Joe Pelle, we typically touch on a current crisis he is facing.

Several years ago Joe introduced me to an enlightening resource. We even hosted a seminar for the cops in our region featuring Kevin Gilmartin, author of *Emotional Survival for Law Enforcement*. That's where I learned about the emotional toll of hypervigilance.

Those facing heavy challenges and even threats are always on full alert at work. When they're off duty, they typically crash. It's confusing to them and to all who love them. How is it possible to be so engaging and aware when on duty but so zoned out when off duty at home? The spouses of those both in law enforcement and in ministry often face this confusion. Why is the one they love so often distant and disconnected?

When I've shared this pattern with pastors, everyone can relate. It's possible to be physically present during a family dinner and yet emotionally absent. It's the price of leadership. I once shared this theme with twenty pastors serving in the slums of Nairobi. They, too, saw the same pattern as they dealt with nonstop deprivation, addiction, and danger. While they energetically served their congregations, they often had little energy left to share with their own families.

As we talked about the danger of living with hypervigilance in the slums, everyone knew they needed help and hope. This is what motivated the overseers among them to launch small covenant groups for soul strength.

Limits are among God's gifts to us all: physical limits, opportunity limits, even emotional limits. No leader will ever thrive without others who understand what leading in tough times is really like. You don't need a lot of people to do that. You just need the right people—people who have the credibility to remind you to acknowledge your limits, as boundaries are good for your soul.

REFLECTION QUESTIONS

When have you paid the price for venturing "out of your lane"?

Who are your most loyal critics and wisest advisers?

How is God teaching you the blessing of boundaries?

CHAPTER 9

PURSUE THE BIGGER YES

"I LONG TO ACCOMPLISH A GREAT AND NOBLE TASK,
BUT IT IS MY CHIEF DUTY TO ACCOMPLISH HUMBLE
TASKS AS THOUGH THEY WERE GREAT AND NOBLE."

—HELEN KELLER

My plans for the next day changed with a simple text. My best friend from Savannah asked if I could meet him at the Denver airport for breakfast before he left on a family vacation in Colorado. My one word response was an emphatic one: "Absolutely!"

The reason I immediately set aside my previous plans was a simple one: I suddenly had a "bigger yes" burning inside me—a strong compelling that seizes me and becomes the top priority for me. Some days are like that, when we experience an unexpected life-enriching opportunity that suddenly changes everything for the better.

Few people in my life lift my spirits more than my friend of fifty years, Cam Huxford. As Paul once said of his young protégé, Timothy, "I have no one else like [him]" (Philippians 2:20).

It's been said that you can't go out and make old friends; you either have them or you don't! I'm blessed to have many good friends, both old and new. Virtually all of them have been been made the same way . . . slowly. I have cultivated those friendships over the years by making time for my friends as they have made time for me. This I know: if you don't make time for your friends, you won't have any. Friends are always part of the "bigger yes" of my life.

My work is all relational. At times that can definitely be inconvenient and even exhausting, but more than anything it is deeply fulfilling. I know that this is what I am called to do, namely to encourage Christian leaders and especially to connect them with one another. This is my passion, it's my "bigger yes."

We all need to heed the prompt of God and at times even the encouragement of God's people to faithfully pursue it. As my friend Ross Runnels once said, "I'm a pretty good dog when it comes to chasing squirrels. I just need my team to remind me which squirrel I should be chasing!"

Someone once said that to leave a lasting legacy we must live for something definite. My definite desire is to end the soul-crushing burden of isolation with which so many struggle. I know firsthand that the isolated leader is the vulnerable leader. I'm out to help change that, and almost every day God gives me the privilege of catalyzing life-enriching connections for others. This is deeply gratifying.

Over the years I've labeled this great sense of compelling as the "bigger yes." I believe there is no substitute for having an unshakable sense of oughtness that a certain something must be addressed . . . now!

YOU HAVE A SPECIAL ASSIGNMENT TOO

What is your "bigger yes"? And do those closest to you know what it is? Once again, the apostle Paul has said something about this: "But you, Timothy, certainly know what I teach, and how I live, and what my purpose in life is. You know my faith, my patience, my love, and my endurance" (2 Timothy 3:10). We all need to see ourselves, and to be seen by our vital few, as devoted to something that is bigger than ourselves.

- What is that for you?
- Who are those for you?

What's your special assignment? We recently enjoyed a four-hour visit with an inspiring couple we have grown to love over the years as we have watched them grow in joyful generosity. We count them among our true heroes. As the psalmist said, "The godly people in the land are my true heroes! I take pleasure in them!" (Psalm 16:3).

Those who enjoy hero status for us all live with a sense of assignment and have three things in common:

- Longtime obedience
- Deep joy
- Strong generosity

"A hero," wrote author Joseph Campbell, "is someone who has given his life to something bigger than himself." After a great meal our relaxing conversation led to Del, one of our true heroes, smiling and saying, "I like to make money so that I can give it away!"

He, like me, is enjoying the high privilege of knowing what he is called to do. Again, I'm inspired by the psalmist: "LORD, you have assigned me my portion and my cup; you have made my lot secure. The boundary lines have fallen for me in pleasant places; surely I have a delightful inheritance" (Psalm 16:5–6 NIV 1984).

All of God's assignments are good ones, and all come with certain boundaries. I definitely don't have the money-making gift that my buddy has, but then again, he would readily admit that he doesn't have my gifts either. Maybe that's why we have enjoyed such a great partnership over the years. We celebrate each other's God-given assignments. And it's those divine assignments that keep us energized and give us a reason to lean into the future.

It's been said that your vision is whatever you'd delay going to heaven in order to accomplish—that's the ultimate "bigger yes." The Message version of the Bible puts 1 Timothy 1:1 this way: "I, Paul, am an apostle on special assignment for Christ, our living hope."

Do you have a sense that you are on special assignment, that something important has been given to you to do—a calling that matters?

LIVING A "SUMMONED" LIFE

New York Times columnist David Brooks suggested that there are two ways of thinking about life: "the Well-Planned Life" and "the Summoned Life."[45] As an avid planner I've been daily gripped with that distinction. What does it matter if my life is consumed with accomplishments if they're not in keeping with my special assignment?

C.S. Lewis once observed that a man's greatest dignity is not found in initiative but in response. In a sense we are all to live in response to the grace of God. These assignments, be they large or small, are ultimately more of a blessing than a burden. Living with a sense of summons is ennobling and inspiring.

When I have a sense that I'm on divine assignment, that "bigger yes" changes everything! I was sitting with several pastor friends taking turns confessing our deepest fears. One man's words really resonated with me. He said, "My greatest fear is not simply falling into immorality of some sort, but failing to fulfill the assignment God has given to me, and failing to seize the opportunities God has set before me."

The ultimate calling of us all is to respond to the summons of the "bigger yes" assignment God has for us. However, sometimes that is more than a little confusing.

For example, I never wanted to be a missionary. I'm one of those who literally prayed, "Lord, please don't send me to Africa!" That was during my early high school years, and it was a genuine concern of mine for some reason, not that anybody was trying to get me to go to Africa. I was just afraid that one day "someone"—i.e., God—might!

As a scrawny Chicago kid, I never pictured myself tromping through the African bush wearing a pith helmet and carrying an elephant gun. I hated the very thought of going to Africa; maybe that's why it haunted me so much.

Back in those days my view of God's will was more than a little twisted. Sometimes I figured that if I *didn't* want to do something, that must be a sure and certain sign that God *did* want me to do it! So I remember exactly where I was when I finally relented and actually prayed out loud in my tiny upstairs bedroom, "Okay, Lord, if that's what you want, I'll even go to Africa!"

Almost instantaneously, the answer came. It was remarkable. It was one of the most clarifying answers to prayer that I've ever received. I didn't hear a voice, but I immediately had relief. I was suddenly freed from my inner angst and clearly sensed that God didn't want me to go to Africa after all. Rather, God just wanted me to be *willing* to go to Africa!

Well, fast-forward several decades and guess what? I've made multiple mission trips, three of them to Africa! As the apostle Paul wrote, "For God is working in you, giving you the desire and the power to do what pleases him" (Philippians 2:13).

I have no doubt that God is working in my life and in yours. He is the one prompting and empowering us to do a variety of things we never would have entertained on our own. God has called us all to Himself through Jesus Christ and called us on purpose. We are His disciples.

As John Stott points out in his little book *The Radical Disciple,* "It comes as a surprise to many people to discover that the followers of Jesus Christ are called 'Christians' only three times in the New Testament."[46] However, the more common term is *disciple,* and to be identified as a disciple of Jesus implies a personal relationship with Jesus.

Interestingly, during the three years of His public ministry, the Twelve were disciples before they were "apostles" or "sent-out ones." And being disciples meant that they were under the instruction of their teacher and Lord, or "under discipline." Whenever a person freely responds to the gospel, he or she is committing to be under discipline or under authority or under orders.

Now *that* is a summoned life.

YOU CAN LIVE A SUMMONED LIFE—AND STILL DOUBT

I find it striking that even after the resurrection of Jesus some of the early disciples doubted. It's recorded in Matthew 28:16–17.

Then the eleven disciples left for Galilee, going to the mountain where Jesus had told them to go. When they saw him, they worshiped him—but some of them doubted!

Now, why and exactly what did the early disciples doubt? We're not told. Obviously, they didn't doubt that Jesus had been crucified; they certainly knew the reality of that. Neither did they doubt that Jesus was alive and standing before them in living color. There was no mistaking that He was actually there. So what was their problem anyway?

Clearly, their doubts had to do with them rather than with Him. Let's face it, they had to have some uncertainty about their future; after all, since Jesus had been crucified, what might be in store for them, as disciples of Jesus? Might it be that they actually doubted that Jesus was still going to be with them through the challenging days ahead? Isn't that at the root of our doubt as well?

It's not that we doubt that God is God. It's that we wonder whether or not we are going to be up to the challenges God is putting before us! Truthfully, that's the story of my life, and it may be your story as well.

At times everyone wrestles with a lack of clarity and confidence. We all wrestle with doubts about tomorrow or the day after, doubts about next month or next year. No one can ever fully know what the future holds. Only God knows the future and He's not telling. "The LORD our God has secrets known to no one. We are not accountable for them" (Deuteronomy 29:29).

If we're waiting until we have a full understanding of every ramification of every commitment, we will never commit to anything. For example, the very reason that marriage vows are made is that commitment is necessary for the fulfillment of them. The same is true in our relationship with Christ.

Until we make a heartfelt commitment to follow Him, we will be immobilized. Until there is commitment, there is always hesitancy. Yet, when there is commitment, there is increasing certainty—not certainty about everything, just about the next thing.

God lights our path one step at a time! In the classic *A Diary of Private Prayer,* John Baillie, wrote this for the twenty-seventh day:

> When the way seems dark before me, give me grace
> to walk trustingly:
> When much is obscure to me, let me be all the more
> faithful to the little that I can clearly see:
> When the distant scene is clouded, let me rejoice that
> at least the next step is plain:
> When what Thou art is most hidden from my eyes,
> let me still hold fast to what Thou dost command:
> When insight falters, let obedience stand firm:
> What I lack in faith let me repay in love.[47]

The key line for me: "When the distant scene is clouded, let me rejoice that at least the next step is plain."

You may be the type who is bold enough to declare a grand life plan. You may even do so expecting it will unfold over the decades without pain or failure, without delay or even difficulty. But never is that the case.

YOU CAN LIVE A SUMMONED LIFE—AND EXPERIENCE HARDSHIP

The Scripture makes it plain that difficulties are to be expected. "Everyone who wants to live a godly life in Christ Jesus will suffer" (2 Timothy 3:12). For some, the hardships and suffering may involve severe persecution and even martyrdom. For many, the suffering will be tears and misunderstandings, betrayal and abandonment, heartache and hard financial times.

It's been said that a season of suffering is worth enduring for a clearer vision of God. We don't get to choose the assignments; we only get to choose our attitude in them and toward them. We certainly don't get to select the sufferings that will accompany them.

But whatever we suffer as a result of our commitment to Christ is suffered on purpose for Christ. That's what makes the calling of the disciple so demanding, so fulfilling, and so rewarding. It's embracing the calling of the next immediate opportunity. That's the calling simply to be a disciple and to shine light right where we are.

All too often we fail to see that the divine moment is the present moment. And the divine assignment is the present assignment, no matter how small or insignificant it might appear to be.

Uncertainty and hardship are inescapable. But these things should never stop us from making a commitment to do what we know God is assigning us to do next. The apostle Paul addresses this very issue in Acts 20:22–24. The context of chapter 20 is based on what just happened in chapter 19. As you may recall, Paul was preaching and a riot broke out. Then after the riot, this line appears in Acts 20:1 (NIV), "When the uproar had ended."

That's very encouraging. Sooner or later all uproars end. However, in verse 3 we read that three months later there was yet another plot to kill Paul, so he returned another way. In other words, in Paul's experience he was either coming out of uproar, in the middle of uproar, or heading into uproar! And the same is often true for any who dare to make a commitment to a ministry of a "bigger yes."

Uproar of some sort is typical. That's life, especially life in leadership. But in Paul's case that didn't keep him from fulfilling his commitment. Here's more from Paul's experience recorded in Acts 20: "And now I am bound by the Spirit to go to Jerusalem. I don't know what awaits me, except that the Holy Spirit tells me in city after city that jail and suffering lie ahead. But my life is worth nothing to me unless I use it for finishing the work assigned me by the Lord Jesus—the work of tell-

ing others the Good News about the wonderful grace of God"
(Acts 20:22–24).

In verse 22 Paul admits to uncertainty about what was in
store for him. But in verse 24, Paul makes it clear that he was
convinced he was on assignment to share the good news. Even
Paul had a lack of clarity, but that didn't mean he had a lack of
commitment. He was still gripped with the "bigger yes" of what
he needed to do.

EMBRACING YOUR ASSIGNMENT

What is it that you are gripped by? Wess Stafford, former
leader of Compassion International, once said, "If you don't
have a cause you can define in thirty seconds or less, you are not
fully alive!" Can you do that?

Do you have any sense of assignment in your life? While
every believer is called to follow Christ, not every believer is
assigned to do the same things. Our assignments are as different
as we are. But this I know: there are no easy assignments left.
The only ones left are the hard ones—that's because all the easy
ones have already been taken! In truth, we all face some difficult challenges at times, especially those that carry significant
responsibilities. And ultimately, the assignments we have from
God are not determined by us; they are only discovered by us.
That is, as servants we don't get to pick them; assignments are
just that: they are assigned.

Paul was convinced that his assignment was to go to Jerusalem on purpose. His purpose was to share the gospel, even though he knew that jail and suffering awaited him. Paul was in essence saying, "I am going to do what I'm called to do, and ought to do, even though in my flesh I don't want to do it."

Let's be honest, most of the difficult assignments in life are given to people who never volunteered for them. Maybe they are even frightened in the face of them. Who in his right mind would want to face jail time and suffering? Paul didn't desire that, but he did desire doing the will of God; he was gripped by that.

What are you gripped by? That may be a clue about your next assignment. Time and again I have been gripped by something I needed to do, even though I didn't want to do it. A hard conversation, a sin confrontation, a faith-stretching mission. Someone once said, "Most of the greatest things in the world were accomplished by people who didn't want to do them. But they saddled up anyway!"

There are always some hard things we simply must do whether we really feel like it or not. For many years my dad went to work in a Chicago factory, not because it was easy but because it was necessary. I watched him courageously face his fears as he worked with both toxic chemicals and toxic people for years, even though he often went to work with a knot in his stomach and a lump in his throat. He did that because he had commitments to fulfill.

As Oswald Chambers noted, "Drudgery is the touchstone of character. The great hindrance in spiritual life is that we will look for big things to do. 'Jesus took a towel . . . and began to wash the disciples' feet.'"

Core commitments can be very clarifying. The hardest things I have faced in ministry and the most tearful times have always brought me back to my core commitment. As Os Guinness said, "First and foremost we are called to Someone, not to something or to somewhere."

Could it be that the next assignment for each of us will be a small one, not a big one, at least in the eyes of the world? I heard a man in one of my groups share how he made a commitment to Christ in college and then made a commitment to ministry, but he choked up as he told of his dad's disapproval and even disdain. His dad was very disappointed that his son had made a commitment to ministry rather than to business, repeatedly telling him, "When are you going to get a real job?!" The absence of his father's blessing was the price he paid for the blessing of his Father in heaven.

These days we have made an idol out of being significant in the eyes of the world, rather than humbly serving the One who is most significant. Too many times we are only willing to step up and serve if we get to pick the inspiring assignment! What if our next assignment doesn't turn out to be a really big one?

Without that core commitment to say no to self and yes to Christ, there will always be hesitancy to accept the next assignment. I believe God has assignments for us all; some are big and some are small. As Mother Teresa was fond of saying, "We cannot all do great things, but we can do small things with great love."

While our time table is temporal, God's time table is eternal. God is rarely in a hurry. Joseph certainly discovered that: "Until the time came to fulfill his dreams, the LORD tested Joseph's character" (Psalm 105:19).

No one makes one single, big commitment that lasts a lifetime without a series of small daily recommitments along the way. The daily commitments of your life define your life. You see, God's blessing rests not merely upon those who make a commitment but upon those who keep a commitment! This may not be something that ever appears on our résumé, but it may become a lasting part of our legacy.

What is the "bigger yes" commitment, be it great or small, that is gripping you now? For your soul's sake, now is the time to choose between the vital one and the trivial many!

REFLECTION QUESTIONS

Have you ever had the sense that you were being summoned to a "bigger yes"?

What are three marks of those you count as your true heroes?

How have you seen a burden become a blessing in your life?

CHAPTER 10

LIVE GRATEFULLY

"THOUGH THE FIG TREE DOES NOT BUD AND THERE
ARE NO GRAPES ON THE VINES, THOUGH THE OLIVE
CROP FAILS AND THE FIELDS PRODUCE NO FOOD,
THOUGH THERE ARE NO SHEEP IN THE PEN AND NO
CATTLE IN THE STALLS, YET I WILL REJOICE IN THE
LORD, I WILL BE JOYFUL IN GOD MY SAVIOR."

—HABAKKUK 3:17-18 NIV

One of the most influential people in my life is my trusted assistant, Judy, who served alongside me for decades. Although sometimes she endured much and faced many challenges, she often repeated the same refrain: "Thank you, God! Thank you, God! Thank you, God!"

Rarely have I heard her express even a hint of complaint. Instead, what I repeatedly hear from her is gratitude, and attitudes of gratitude are not only inspiring; they're infectious!

It's been noted that the two most frequent prayers are "Please help!" and "Thank you!" Those are wonderful prayers, but what if we have them reversed? What if "Thank you" should come before "Please help?" I read one time that with prayers of gratitude, you can thank your way right into the presence of God.

"May the peoples praise you, O God; may all the peoples praise you. The land yields its harvest, and God, our God, blesses us" (Psalm 67:5–6 NIV).

Could it be that praise precedes plenty?

GRATITUDE ISN'T ABOUT THE "EASY" LIFE

Most people I talk with these days have some sort of hard story to tell. "It's a hard-knock life for us." You may remember the line from *Little Orphan Annie*. Then again you may resonate with it from your own experience. In fact, while most of the leaders I know are very good with words, some struggle to find the best words to express why they're feeling so tired right now.

One of my exhausted buddies recently asked this question: "Are you coming across pastors who are struggling with the 'new normal'? I know I sure am. How did you gut it out to the finish line?"

I responded by saying that while I didn't have the "new normal" to deal with, I did have the same as he did: a high calling!

A clear and compelling sense of calling is key for us all. I've discovered that if you have a clear and compelling sense of purpose, you can handle just about anything.

Once again, all the easy positions have been taken. The only ones left are assignments like yours. Yes, while leading a noble and hopeful life as a parent, pastor, teacher, business owner, or police officer is definitely a tough assignment, it's not the only tough one.

No one has a monopoly on hard. Most everyone is living their own version of hard right now. I'm in near daily conversations with leaders feeling overwhelming stress. One just told me that he's never had so much trouble sleeping. Another said he was exhausted by unrelenting challenges hitting his inbox and iPhone all day every day, even on weekends.

Everyone seems to be tired and longing for relief. I think I know why—it's the unrelenting uncertainty of our times. Uncertainty is exhausting!

In ministry and in leadership roles of any sort, you're either coming out of a crisis, in the middle of a crisis, or heading into a crisis. In some ways that's inevitable, and it's what the apostle Paul reminds us: "we must suffer many hardships to enter the Kingdom of God" (Acts 14:22). It's similar to what Jesus tells us: "Here on earth you will have many trials and sorrows" (John 16:33).

Could it be that we are all a little naive, or entitled, or spoiled due to unrealistic expectations?

WE DON'T HAVE A MONOPOLY ON "HARD"

When I first read *Undaunted Courage* by Steven Ambrose, I was both humbled and inspired. It's the account of the Lewis and Clark expedition to the Pacific Northwest in 1805–1807. I read the book again last summer as Linda and I enjoyed the Columbia and Snake Rivers Cruise tracing their epic journey. The challenges they faced were astonishing, and they had no way of properly preparing for them. They simply had to press on and keep moving forward, far from the comfort and fine dining of a cruise ship!

We watched the John Adams series again on PBS about the life and times of our second president. It's humbling to see the suffering and sacrifice of those leading during the early days of our nation and the Revolutionary War. Back then, normal life, even for most leaders, was miserable by the standards of our time.

I noted the same thing in the book entitled *The Boys in the Boat: The True Story of an American Team's Epic Journey to Win Gold at the 1936 Olympics.* That success shocked the world and was set against the backdrop of the Great Depression and the looming threat of Nazi Germany. Most people were at best just eking out a living, and yet some still managed to lead others to high performance in the midst of high stress.

In the riveting book *The Choice: Embrace the Possible,* Dr. Edith Eva Eger shares her own story as a survivor of Auschwitz. After enduring unspeakable horrors, she went on both to survive and to thrive by shifting her focus. She refused to succumb to self-pity and bitterness and as a result is no longer a hostage to the past. She is no longer the prisoner of anything. She said, "I am free!"

While there has never been a time like ours, there have definitely been harder times than ours. What we know is that high stress and hard knocks have been common since the garden of Eden.

While we endured the serious challenge of the COVID virus, it wasn't the worst ever epidemic of all time. During the 1918 flu epidemic, at least fifty million people died worldwide and about 675,000 in the U.S. Guess what? Parents still had to support their families, medical people still had to serve the sick, and pastors still had to lead funerals during the week and share messages of hope on Sundays.

YES, YOU CAN EXPERIENCE HARDSHIP, BLESSING, AND GRATITUDE—AT THE SAME TIME!

Hard knocks are inevitable . . . but then so are blessings. These days I prefer to encourage those I serve to remember that we are either coming out of a season of unspeakable blessing, in the middle of a season of unspeakable blessing, or heading into a season of unspeakable blessing. While hard is inevitable, so is the blessing of the presence of God.

During the hardest seasons of my life in leadership, it always helped me to remember that I was on special assignment.

I not only chose to be a pastor, I knew I was called to be a pastor. Whatever your hard assignment happens to be, you are not alone. Others are with you, and some are setting an inspiring pace and example for you. One of the younger leaders of one of our largest churches did that for me.

Kyle Idleman talked about the overlapping challenges his congregation was facing in Louisville, Kentucky. Speaking to those in his church of twenty thousand (a congregation composed of many in law enforcement and of various ethnicities), Kyle spoke warmly of his gratitude. He talked about how grateful he was to be a pastor during this hard time because of his privilege to share encouragement and hope.

This I know: those who radiate the most hope always lead best. That's especially true during hard times! As my longtime assistant knows firsthand and has often reminded me and others facing challenges, "With Christ in you, you are stronger than you think you are . . . you can do more than you think you can . . . and you are loved more than you could ever know."

Never doubt that, in Christ, you are more loved and blessed than you know!

A good friend shared a series of messages entitled "The Genius of Gratitude." When Bryan Myers and I brainstormed about that theme, we each began to celebrate some of what we've learned about this life-giving truth about the benefits of gratitude in our own lives. But then shortly after a long call he texted me with a further request for help. He wanted me to email an illustration I had shared earlier. I was in the middle of other things and honestly wasn't exactly "grateful" for the interruption!

Ironic, isn't it? Here we were, gripped with the theme of gratitude, and then a few hours later I was bothered by his request to shoot him a quick email. So I didn't do it. I called so he could actually hear me groan for a few moments before quickly dictating it once again. That wasn't good enough. He pleaded with me to write it out for him! Whew, friends aren't always convenient!

Sometimes I'm a "reluctant blesser." That is, sometimes I'm a little too preoccupied, distracted, or tired to provide help cheerfully. But then, after I help, I usually end up more than gratified. Maybe you can relate. Well, now I'm truly grateful again, and I think it was ingenious of Bryan to bug me to find the illustration. Here it is.

I read of a study in which people were randomly assigned to three groups and asked to journal five things daily.

- Group 1 was asked to focus on five major challenges.
- Group 2 was asked to focus on five minor hassles.
- Group 3 was asked to focus on five reasons for gratitude.

While people were randomly assigned to the various groups, the results were amazing. As we might predict, the gratitude group became the most grateful. But even more notable, the gratitude group was most likely to help others.

In short, reflecting and journaling with gratefulness resulted in individuals in the assigned group all becoming more energetic, hopeful, and helpful. The more grateful people had the greatest emotional capacity to help other people! This is absolutely essential for those seeking to influence others for good.

GRATITUDE IS A GAME CHANGER

I have been journaling for years. Sadly, sometimes I have recorded too many sad things. While at times that has been emotionally cathartic, more often it has been emotionally depleting and spiritually restricting. In fact, if anyone found some of my old journals, they might marvel that I wasn't institutionalized! That's why I've changed my journaling ways.

Guess what? Daily, for the last few years, I've recorded five things that have prompted me to express gratitude to God. I'm finding that the more I focus my prayers in praise, the more reasons I see to celebrate the goodness of God. In short, I'm magnifying Him and not my problems.

What do you want to magnify? While prayer alone, or journaling alone, or reflecting alone may at times magnify problems, praise only magnifies God. "I will bless the Lord at all times; his praise shall continually be in my mouth. . . . Oh, magnify the Lord with me, and let us exalt his name together!" (Psalm 34:1, 3 ESV).

So, what are the things you are grateful for . . . today? If listing five seems too daunting, just start with two or three. A leader of another covenant group took this idea and started his own "Grateful 4" practice. Adam Turner writes four things every day that have brought him delight. King David wrote, "Let all that I am praise the LORD; may I never forget the good things he does for me" (Psalm 103:2).

I've long loved and recommended the classic book *In a Pit with a Lion on A Snowy Day* by Mark Batterson. Every man I've ever given it to loved it and thought the book was written just for him. Here's just a snippet: "I think there are basically two types of people in the world: complainers and worshipers. And there isn't much circumstantial difference between the two. Complainers will always find something to complain about. Worshipers will always find something to praise God about. They simply have different default settings."[48]

What's your default setting? When I'm tired or drained, I can easily slip into an audible groan. It can happen with a computer glitch, a phone call of interruption, a traffic jam, or a bad news story via the media.

Even though I sometimes like to moan and groan, I never like how it messes with my mind and heart. Even when moaning a bit doesn't leave me entirely miserable, it still saps my emotional energy. By contrast, every time I think and talk about good things, my spirit is lifted.

My words shape my world all the time. That's why I've challenged groups to memorize and regularly recite together Philippians 4:4–9 (NIV):

> Rejoice in the LORD always. I will say it again: Rejoice! Let your gentleness be evident to all. The LORD is near. Do not be anxious about anything, but in every situation, by prayer and petition, with thanksgiving present your requests to God. And the peace of God, which transcends all understanding, will guard your hearts and minds in Christ Jesus.
>
> Finally, brothers and sisters, whatever is true, whatever is noble, whatever is right, whatever is pure, whatever is lovely, whatever is admirable—if anything is excellent or praiseworthy—think about such things. Whatever you have learned or received or heard from me, or seen in me—put it into practice. And the God of peace will be with you.

The man who wrote those words has unmatched credibility. The apostle Paul penned this when in prison, chained by the wrist to a Roman guard. Therefore, he has the moral authority to tell you and me to quit whining and to start rejoicing. If he can choose to rejoice, we can too!

Paul was living under the threat of a death sentence, and so are we all. No one gets out of this world alive unless Jesus returns first. We all have a limited number of days but a limitless opportunity to rejoice in the One who redeems all things.

Monica Brands, a content editor with Our Daily Bread Ministries said, "I'm captivated by how author Frederick Buechner describes God's grace: like a gentle voice that says, 'Here is the world. Terrible and beautiful things will happen. Don't be afraid. I am with you.'"

Yes, bad stuff happens and even worse. There will never be a day without tons of bad stuff to take note of. Neither will there ever be a day without beautiful things to celebrate and to be grateful for.

It's been said that the worst day for an atheist is feeling grateful and having no one to thank! That's not our problem. We're told, "Every good and perfect gift is from above, coming down from the Father of the heavenly lights" (James 1:17 NIV). We all have multiple reasons for gratitude every day. Our problem is failing to pause and to take note of them. Then, having noted them, to sincerely thank God for them.

What gifts do you daily thank God for? I thank God daily for numerous things and people, specifically having

- Someone special to love
- Something significant to do
- Something wonderful to look forward to

Even though I am immensely grateful, I ask God to make me more grateful still! After Daniel was hauled off to a foreign land in Babylonian captivity, he went to his room, knelt, and thanked God three times a day. Something happens in my spirit when I do that.

The very act of kneeling and expressing thankfulness changes me by moving me to a better place, mentally and spiritually. I now choose to do this multiple times a day, most every day. But when I don't, I notice the difference.

One of the classic auditions for *America's Got Talent* wrecked me. A radiant young woman named Jane (stage name Night Bird) introduced an original song, "It's Okay"—a story about the prior year of her life. Before she sang, she was asked if anyone had come to the show with her. She said, "No, I'm here by myself."

She was asked what she did for a living. She said that she had not been working for quite a few years as she'd been dealing with cancer. When asked how she was doing, she said, "The last time I checked I have some cancer in my lungs, my spine, and my liver."

A judge said, "So you're not okay. . . . You've got a beautiful smile and glow. Nobody would know!"

To that she said, "It's important that everyone knows I'm so much more than the bad things that happen to me . . . You can't wait until life isn't hard anymore until you decide to be happy."

When asked how it was going, she said, "They give me a two percent chance . . . but it's okay, two percent isn't zero percent."

Her song was profound because her presentation was stunningly personal. After a breathtaking pause at the end, everyone jumped to their feet with a powerful ovation. After that, Simon slammed the Golden Buzzer, and she was literally enveloped with beautiful blessings of gold confetti released from above!

Gratitude begets gratitude. The psalmist reminds us, "This is the day the LORD has made. We will rejoice and be glad in it" (Psalm 118:24). Here's a beautiful reading by Gregory M. Lousignont that serves as my Bible marker for this passage:

> Today when I awoke I suddenly realized this was going to be the best day of my life ever. There were times when I wondered if I would make it to today, but I did. And because I did, I'm going to celebrate. Today I'm going to celebrate what an unbelievable life I've had so far. The accomplishments, the many blessings and, yes, even the hardships, because they have served to make me stronger. I will go through this day with my head held high and a happy heart. I will marvel at God's seemingly simple gifts, the morning dew, the sun, the clouds the trees, the flowers, the birds. Today none of the miraculous creations will escape my notice. Today I will share my excitement for life with other people. I will make someone smile. I will go out of my way to perform an unexpected act of kindness for someone I don't even know. Today I'll give a sincere compliment to someone who seems down.

Today is the day that I'll quit worrying about what I don't have and start being grateful for all the wonderful things that God has already given to me. I'll remember that to worry is just a waste of time because my faith in God and His divine plan ensures everything will be just right. And then tonight, before I go to bed, I'll go outside and raise my eyes to the heavens. I'll stand in awe at the beauty of the stars and the moon and I will praise God for these magnificent treasures. As the day ends I will lay my head down on my pillow. I will thank the Almighty, the Lord Jesus Christ, for the best day of my life and I will sleep the sleep of a contented child, excited with expectation because I know tomorrow is going to be the best day of my life ever.

There will never be a better time to press pause and praise God than right now.

- In the middle of your mess, thank God for the Messiah!
- In the middle of uncertainty, thank God for the Redeemer!
- In the middle of conflict, thank God for His presence!

WRITE IT DOWN

Someone has observed that praise is often much more powerful than prayer. That's because prayer can be filled with self-pity and fear, while praise is filled with faith. I can relate to that. When I praise God, I find it liberating and energizing. That often happens best when I have a pen in hand and write some of my gratitude discoveries down before I forget them!

This I know: journaling can rewire your brain! That's one of the most powerful lessons I've learned in recent years. I once used my journal space to scribble about frustrations or difficulties. Now I find that focusing on gratitude improves my disposition and writing what I'm grateful for improves my memory!

You're probably not as smart as you think you are. Studies are now documenting that computers are not making us smarter. In fact, it's just the opposite. It turns out that the act of physically writing things down helps us to remember things better. Yes, that means actually writing longhand with a pen.

The New York Times article "What's Lost as Handwriting Fades" quotes Stanislaw Dehaene, psychologist at College de France, on handwriting versus keyboarding: "When we write, a unique neural circuit is automatically activated. There is a core recognition of the gesture in the written word, a sort of recognition by mental simulation in your brain. And it seems this circuit is contributing in unique ways we didn't realize. Learning is made easier."[49] I find that intriguing. In this day of technological addiction we are losing our capacity for retention. Many don't even think that physically writing much of anything is really important anymore. Think again.

While computers can retrieve information for us, computers cannot reflect. As the psalmist himself said, "I pondered the direction of my life" (Psalm 119:59). How long has it been since you *pondered* something? Well, if you're ready to enjoy the benefits of reflecting and retaining, you need to pick up a pen and write!

I've written daily entries in my journal for decades. Here's how it helps me:

- Writing helps me to capture insights. My thoughts disentangle themselves when they pass through my fingertips.
- Writing forces me to slow down. Writing helps to free me from frantic feelings.
- Writing forces me to be honest. My rationalizations seem to stand out when I see them staring back at me in black and white.
- Writing rejuvenates me. As I reflect on the past and plan for the future, I enjoy both closure and clarity.

A close friend lamented that he had no time to ponder. I challenged him, on the spot, to pull out his notepad and immediately begin writing a few things down. He did it and discovered that beginning is a huge incentive to continuing!

Leaders are both writers and readers and therefore are better "rememberers." I found a fascinating bit of biblical instruction given by God to the king of Israel: "When he sits on the throne as king, he must copy for himself this body of instruction on a scroll in the presence of the Levitical priests. He must always keep that copy with him and read it daily as long as he lives" (Deuteronomy 17:18–19).

The Lord commanded the kings to do their daily devotions from the Scriptures copied by their own hands. Might there be something here for each of us to heed? Writing anything helps us to remember better.

As I'm finishing this book, I've been gripped by the words of the apostle Peter: "so I will work hard to make sure you always remember these things after I am gone" (2 Peter 1:15).

What good things do you want others to remember from you for the years to come? If you want to grow in gratitude, and leave a lasting legacy, start writing them down, right now!

REFLECTION QUESTIONS

Who has best modeled gratitude for you?

How does social media affect your attitude?

What has most recently sparked gratitude for you?

CHAPTER 11

FINISH WITH BLESSING

"GREAT IS THE ART OF BEGINNING, BUT GREATER
IS THE ART OF ENDING."

—HENRY WADSWORTH LONGFELLOW

I called up a friend *for* lunch and then I called him up *over* lunch! By that I mean I encouraged him to see his service as a sort of special assignment from on high.

My friend isn't just frustrated with his job; he is disappointed with the lack of results. Now, if I told you where he worked and what he did, you would admire him. While you definitely wouldn't envy his challenging setting, you would envy his high calling. His role makes him a sort of rock star to many, including me. However, even though he knows that, it's just not enough. He's still tired and would like to quit.

How do you know when it's time to quit?

Believe it or not, most people who enter ministry, even though beginning with great enthusiasm, eventually end up dropping out. The dropout rate is something like 50 percent within the first five years or so, and then it gets worse! Only about 10 percent of those who remain after the initial glow wears off actually remain active in ministry for the full run. Just 10 percent!

In short, most who start well never finish well, at least in that position. Why? At the risk of generalizing too much, let me offer a few reasons:

- Inadequate support: they feel under paid and under affirmed by those they seek to serve.
- Inadequate disciplines: they fail to exercise spiritually and physically.
- Inadequate guardrails: they forget their humanity and naively succumb to the allure of forbidden fruit.
- Inadequate awareness: they forget they have an enemy out to destroy them and all they hold dear.
- Inadequate friendships: they postpone building and servicing deep relationships with others to whom they can safely bare their soul.

The same day I called up my friend over lunch I also called up someone via email. I replied to a leader who is wondering whether he has the bandwidth for a covenant group. It's a big commitment. A three-year commitment should not be entered into lightly.

Once again, the groups like the ones I help to catalyze and lead are for leaders too busy to be in one! So I called him up by asking which season he is currently experiencing:

- Are you just coming out of a season of great challenge?
- Are you in the middle of a season of great challenge?
- Are you heading into a season of great challenge?

Those questions were intended to call him up. I was encouraging him to see that the best time to get ready for a challenge is long before it even begins.

You might not be in ministry. You might not be the CEO of a large company. But whatever your profession or calling, perhaps you are waiting too long to prepare for whatever the future holds. This happens for many of us.

That's true with everything from stocking up on basic essentials, building a retirement nest egg, or investing in healthy friendships. There's a popular Chinese proverb that says, "The best time to plant a tree was twenty years ago. The second best time is now."

I love to be "called up," and I love to do the same for others. We all need the regular reminder that what we do really matters. High callings all begin with the realization that even ordinary jobs and ministries are special assignments. The key is whether they are done *with* Christ and *for* Him.

I need to be regularly "called up." How about you? "May he give you the power to accomplish all the good things your faith prompts you to do" (2 Thessalonians 1:11).

DO YOU NEED TO PREPARE TODAY FOR A TRANSITION DOWN THE ROAD?

One of those good things for you may be accepting that someday, perhaps even someday soon, someone will succeed you! The only question is how well it will go; transitions aren't easy to navigate. Experiencing a healthy transition is often rare for many long-term leaders and their organizations; therefore, humility is essential.

We all have an expiration date. When you think about it, every leader is ultimately an "interim leader" before the next one. Even though it may be many years yet to come, we're all in transition. The question is not *if* but rather *when* and *how* we will leave.

One man I baptized was a former member of the Mafia and was surprisingly adamant about this topic. Not long before my transition from the role of lead pastor at the age of sixty-five, Jim said, "Even in the Mafia we had to have a succession plan. What's yours?"

Let's face it, the best way for a longtime leader, especially the founding pastor, to leave, is being martyred on a mission trip! That may sound dramatic and tragic, but at least it's clear and definite. However, that's not likely to happen; therefore, we need to get ready for a different sort of grief.

Prior to my own transition, I was warned that it would be harder and hurt more than expected. Grief is a complicated thing. However, by God's grace, the grief of any ending can open doors to new opportunities for all. What's essential is for leaders to embrace the transition rather than to resent it.

Grieving while leading is common. Just as there is no perfect leader or organization, there can be no perfect leadership transition. Every church and organization is a unique combination of flawed people and challenging circumstances never to be repeated again.

GRATITUDE WHILE GRIEVING

I've learned that great gratitude is the greatest antidote to great grief. As I see it now, the more problems you have (or have had), the more potential you have to help others. God never wastes a pain. He lights our path one step at a time so that we can help light the path for others. As the psalmist said, "Light shines in the darkness for the godly" (Psalm 112:4).

Timing requires waiting and trusting. Endings can be both sad and scary, but in God's grand plan they can actually become beautiful new beginnings. As someone once said, "A sunset in one land is always a sunrise in another."

Psychologist Henry Cloud's insightful book entitled *Necessary Endings* provides excellent vocabulary that helps us embrace the inevitable:

> Whether we like it or not, endings are part of life. They are woven into the fabric of life itself, both when it goes well and also when it doesn't. On the good side of life, for us to ever get to a new level, a new tomorrow, or the next step, something has to end. Life has seasons, stages and phases. For there to be anything new, old things always have to end, and we have to let go of them. . . . Endings are not only part of life; they are requirement for living and thriving, professionally and personally.[50]

Timely endings are more art than science. There's really no one-size-fits-all approach. Prior to my own transition I searched for insights far and wide and really appreciated the wisdom in several books, including Bob Russell and Bryan Bucher's little book *Transition Plan,* in which the authors recommend four things:

- Find a successor.
- Find a strategy.
- Set a date.
- Share your personal plan.[51]

There's no guarantee that things will ever go according to anyone's plan. I've long leaned on the wisdom of Mother

Teresa's words: "Write your plans in pencil and give God the eraser."

SHOULD YOU BE PREPARING FOR A SUCCESSOR?

The answer to that question is absolutely "yes" for all who want to finish well, even for young leaders just getting started! Transition seasons may come unexpectedly and are filled with the unexpected. Only God knows the future, and He doesn't tell us; He only calls us to trust. Letting go isn't easy, especially for those of us who have taken our calling and responsibilities so seriously for so long. However, when I could see that the church I had loved and led for nearly thirty years was finally stable once again and finally beyond a long series of daunting crises, I knew it was finally time.

Shortly after my transition I found this passage: "I heard an unknown voice say, 'Now I will take the load from your shoulders; I will free your hands from their heavy tasks. You cried to me in trouble, and I saved you'" (Psalm 81:5–7). Those words from Asaph's psalm really resonated with me. It felt as if it were written just for me. Might it also be for you?

Leaving isn't simply a matter of wise planning. On some level, grieving is inevitable. However, letting go is essential for healthy closure. Yet personal readiness must be matched by situational readiness. While some leaders are tempted to stay too long, others are ready far sooner than their ministry may allow.

Until there is a sense of release, the leader must remain for the good of others. A godly leader will never linger simply for his own benefit, but he may need to stay a little longer for the benefit of others. That must be a prayerful and careful decision. It must not be made in isolation. We need the godly counsel of others in discerning God's timing.

Timing is everything. In the Greek language, *chronos time* is calendar time, but *kairos* time is different. *Kairos time* is the defining moment when God reaches in and changes everything. No leader should stay a day too long or desire to leave a day too soon. We must be sensitive to the movement of the Spirit. These moments shouldn't be forced, but by the power of the Holy Spirit they should be seized, especially when others see and sense the same thing.

When one leader of a strong ministry was considering transitioning to another even larger ministry, I made a surprising suggestion. My sense was that the new opportunity would not be a good fit for him and that his current assignment was not yet finished. We both remember when I suggested that, as he approached his tenth anniversary, he "succeed" himself in the same place! To "succeed himself" meant to make a new beginning with a new attitude. For this to happen, Arron needed a new perspective on his leadership role for the next season. That rang true for us both, and as a result he made a fresh start with the same church. That's where he continues to serve with great fulfillment to this very day!

Transitions aren't always a matter of a change in your geographical location. They can also be brought about by a change in your personal disposition. In other words, in some cases your "successor" may be your better self!

The transition zone is always a danger zone. In the transition of a longtime leader, the well-being of both the organization and the leader is at stake; therefore, you can't afford to merely listen to yourself. "Plans go wrong for lack of advice; many advisers bring success" (Proverbs 15:22).

When I was strongly tempted to leave too soon, my closest advisers intervened. One said, "For the sake of your successor you can't leave now!" Another was even stronger: "The voice in your head is not from God!" I'm glad that I leaned on better counsel than my own. I needed wisdom far beyond my own to make a wise decision. "If you listen to constructive criticism, you will be at home among the wise" (Proverbs 15:31).

The commitment of the departing leader must be to God's timing and not merely to his own. For a pastor the call is to love the church by honoring the elders and blessing the socks off of his successor. But it goes both ways. The key is mutual honoring—the outgoing leader needs to feel valued, and the incoming leader needs to feel trusted. People will only "let go" to the degree that the departing pastor and his or her spouse "let go." And people will only happily move forward to the degree that the departing pastor and his or her spouse happily move forward. Note, that doesn't mean that a retiring pastor and family always have to "move away," but they do have to "move forward"!

If you're not a pastor, you may think this doesn't apply to you. Think again. Everyone is in transition; that's life. In the book *The Heroes Farewell: What Happens When CEOs Retire?*, author Jeffrey Sennefeld raises the question, "What kind of leader am I?" Examples he suggests include the following:

- Monarch: "I am the mission!"
- General: "You can't win without me!"
- Governor: "When I've completed my term, I move on."
- Ambassador: He stays as a cheer-leader and advocate for the mission, the team and the successor.[52]

The ideal transition involves mutual blessing between the outgoing leader and his successor. As Jim Collins once observed, "An organization cannot be truly great if it cannot be great without you." In my own season of transition, I told the leaders that I was looking for three key qualities in my successor, and it wasn't merely two out of these three; it was *all* three:

- Character I can trust
- Capabilities I can respect
- Compatibility I can enjoy

I was blessed to find all three in the man God chose to succeed me. It's been nearly a decade since Shan Moyers and I began our partnership, and I've never stopped thanking God for bringing him to me and our ministry at the kairos moment!

While transitions are seasons of great challenge, they are also seasons of wonderful opportunity. In fact, most of the miracles of the Bible are clustered around three transitions: Moses to Joshua, Elijah to Elisha, and Jesus to the apostles.

Timely transitions should not be feared as long as the transitioning leader is well prepared and preparing those around him. As the season of transition approaches, many leaders hesitate and delay for two reasons: they know they must have something to live on, and they know they must have something to live for.

THE END OF ONE ASSIGNMENT, THE BEGINNING OF THE NEXT

Everyone wins when a leader is ready to embrace what's next. A friend with decades as a wealth manager said he has helped hundreds of professionals transition over the years, and while few of them had any real concerns about having enough to live on, most had little to live for!

This is why retirement can be deadly. After a few months of uninterrupted leisure, many people find life empty and unfulfilling. Work is not a penalty. God made us to make a difference.

That's why it's imperative that we continue to live on purpose, with a purpose. Productivity doesn't have to be for a paycheck, but it must be for something beyond oneself.

Certainly, those in ministry know that while we can retire from a calling to a particular position or career, we will never retire from our calling as a Christ follower. The same should be true for every believer.

Sadly, finishing well is rare and can never be taken for granted. I recently discovered some prophetic words in my journal from 1991. Bill Hybels, a pastor highly esteemed by tens of thousands said, "My greatest fear is to end up in the 'DNF' category, 'Did Not Finish!'" Fast-forward. This gifted teacher is no longer anywhere to be seen. After putting on countless leadership clinics over the years, his final clinic was a cautionary tale for all who had ever admired him.

No leader or church is perfect; therefore, there will never be a perfect ending. However, there can be a healthy and God-honoring one. In Bob Buford's book *Finishing Well,* Howard Hendrix is quoted as sharing a study at Fuller Seminary on a hundred leaders in the Bible about whom we have adequate data to evaluate on how they finished. Only one-third finished well, with most of them failing in the last half of life. They didn't fail due to inadequate knowledge of Scripture; rather, they failed for two reasons. First, they failed to apply the Scripture in their lives. Second, they failed to have an accountability group.[53]

Only a minority finish strong. In 2007 the Francis Schaeffer Institute of Church Leadership in Geneva reported that 90 percent of Christian leaders don't finish well. But finishing well doesn't mean that every graph is up and to the right. Rather, as my friend Dr. John Walker says, "Finishing well means to be more in love with Jesus at the end than at the beginning."

Flourishing to the finish line is the key. It doesn't mean serving for a certain number of years in a certain location or role; it's all about relationships. "The righteous will flourish like a palm tree, they will grow like a cedar of Lebanon; planted in the house of the LORD, they will flourish in the courts of our God. They will still bear fruit in old age, they will stay fresh and green" (Psalm 92:12–14 NIV). It's about a growing love relationship with the lover of your soul and a growing love commitment to the Christian community God has called you into.

Author John Bevere concluded that the ideal way to leave a church is summarized in Isaiah: "For you shall go out with joy, and be led out with peace" (Isaiah 55:12 NKJV).

EMBRACE YOUR *NEXT* BIGGER YES!

No one will ever be any richer than their relationships—now and forever. We must never stop longing for what is yet to come. I love the words of Kennon Callahan, who years ago wrote, "The watershed question for many people in many, many congregations is this: 'Do you believe that your best years are behind you, or do you believe that your best years are yet before you?' . . . God is not simply in the past. God is in the present and the future leading and drawing us toward newness of life . . . hope is stronger than memory."

Comedian George Burns died at the age of 99. Shortly before his death he wrote, "There's an old saying, 'Life begins at 40.' That's silly—life begins every morning when you wake up. Open your mind to it; don't just sit there—do things . . . the possibilities are endless. The point is, with a good positive attitude (and a little bit of luck) there's no reason why you can't live to be 100. And once you've done that you've really got it made because very few people die over 100!"

You may not make it to the century mark. In the prayer of Moses recorded in Psalm 90:10 (NIV), he says, "Our days may come to seventy years, or eighty, if our strength endures." I like to say that I am now in my "extra strength" years; that is, I'm fulfilled but I'm not yet finished, and I'm not alone.

A strong business leader of about my age thought he might have another twenty-five years left to live, and observed that twenty-five years is an awesome responsibility! I may not have that long, but even if it's just a decade or so of reasonable energy, I want to make the most of it. We should never underestimate the importance of whatever time we have left.

If you are looking forward to a major transition, may you live until you die. May God grace you with everything you need:

- Enough tears to keep you tender.
- Enough success to keep you encouraged.
- Enough failure to keep you humble.

- Enough faith to keep you believing that the best is yet to be!

It's been said that the Christian life can be summarized in one word: trust.

Jesus said, "I am leaving you with a gift—peace of mind and heart. And the peace I give is a gift the world cannot give. So don't be troubled or afraid" (John 14:27).

The future is nothing to fear. God is already there waiting for you to arrive. As C.S. Lewis once said, "There are far, far better things ahead than any we leave behind."

REFLECTION QUESTIONS

What are your personal marks for finishing well?

Have you ever considered moving on from your current role? What were the factors contributing to your decision?

Has anyone ever helped you by calling you up? Describe the experience.

CHAPTER 12

STOP PROCRASTINATING!

"I WILL GO ANYWHERE, PROVIDED IT IS FORWARD."

—DAVID LIVINGSTON

A friend of ours says that her ninth grade son earned an A+ in procrastination! Most of us know exactly what that is. We've all earned the same grade time and again. We fully intend to schedule that conversation or read that book or start that project, just not right now. Then before we know it, *not right now* becomes *not ever*.

By contrast, there are those people who determine to ignore the distractions and pursue the project no matter what. Men like Nehemiah.

If you'll recall the biblical account, Nehemiah was seized with the need to rebuild the walls of Jerusalem—so much so that he sought the permission of a pagan king to take on the effort. This passionate and purpose-filled man had many adversaries seeking to distract him. Then, at one critical moment re-corded in Nehemiah 6:3 (NIV), he said, "I am carrying on a great project and cannot go down. Why should the work stop while I leave it and go down to you?"

We all live with unrelenting distractions that can combine together to keep us from pursuing God's best. When I was con-victed recently about my own pattern of procrastination in fin-ishing this book, that passage from Nehemiah came to mind. The very next morning I was stabbed by the words of Tim Keller and this question: "Is there a project you have not been able to finish? Stir up your love for the people who would benefit from it, look to the 'finisher' of our faith (Hebrews 12:2 KJV), and finish it."[54]

What if greater love was really the key to seeing something through to completion? At the close of a recent soul care retreat, one of the men made a stunning statement. He humbly said, "I'm repenting of squandering my leadership gift!"

Now, if you knew the special challenges this father of five was facing on the home front, you may have told him not to be so hard on himself. He lives with enormous challenges both in leading his family and his family of faith; however, he came under conviction that he had not been properly leading himself! That's where we all need to focus first.

We must admit that to some extent we are where we are be-cause of poor choices we have made and good opportunities we have squandered. It might be as simple as passively consuming too much media instead of actively pursuing the special assignment God has set before us. In Nehemiah's case, he chose not only to begin a grand project but to see it through to completion in just fifty-two days. That's just slightly more than seven weeks!

What grand project might you be able to start and finish in the next seven weeks? I definitely know what mine is. Do you have one in mind? Some people squander their leadership opportunity by never getting started, others by never getting around to finishing!

GETTING THINGS DONE

As a young church planter in South Carolina, I was befriended by an upper-level business leader. The day I visited his large office, I was shocked by both the size of his staff and the size of his office. Even more amazing to me, his large private office looked like a display in a high-end furniture store. There wasn't even one scrap of paper in sight! I laughed and said, "Don't you ever do any work around here?" Paul smiled and then convicted me by saying, "I learned a long time ago that I can only do one thing at a time!"

Years ago, Charles Schwab confronted a management consultant with an unusual challenge: "Show me a way to get more things done and if it works, I'll pay anything within reason." The consultant then handed him a piece of paper and had him write down the things he needed to do the next day. Then he had him number them in order of priority. Then he said, "Tomorrow begin with item one and don't move on until you've finished it. Then every day do the same thing. Make a list, put things in order of priority and begin at the top. After you've done that for several weeks, just send me a check for whatever you think it's worth."

A few weeks later the consultant received a surprisingly large check with a note from Charles Schwab saying that this little exercise was the most profitable lesson he had ever learned in his entire business career!

You don't have to pay anything for this counsel, but what if you applied it?

- How have you been squandering your own leadership opportunities lately?
- What is the better thing you need to be doing now?
- When will you determine to launch a fifty-two-day project that might change the trajectory of your life, your family, your ministry, or the lives of those you have been called to serve?

There will never be a day without distractions, nor a day without the opportunity to repeatedly begin again! A work in progress is still progress. Something is better than nothing. We can't do it all, but we can do something by starting now!

CHOOSING THE BETTER THING

I can't encourage you enough to stop procrastinating and start choosing the better thing.

And one of the best things you can choose to do is intentionally create environments and embrace relationships that will strengthen your soul.

We don't just need another book, conference, or academic degree. We need to know in the center of our soul that we are known, loved, and accepted.

That's the key to thriving!

For myself—and hundreds of leaders I've worked with—a key to thriving has been found in covenant groups. These soul-enriching small groups create the opportunity for connection, authenticity, growth, and transformation.

Whether you visit covenant-connections.org and launch your own covenant group, or join or launch a small group under a different model, connections that go deep will be the secret sauce to any transformation you long to make in your life.

Unfortunately, getting started with a small group is one of those things that is easy to put off. It rarely feels like an urgency for anyone. That's why many postpone it . . . indefinitely! It's not because they don't intend to do it *someday*; it's just that the ideal day rarely arrives.

One reason we so often procrastinate is because we don't know exactly what to do, or how to do it, or whom to ask to join us. Often those ready and willing to start a group hesitate because they've never actually led a group designed to connect with both head and heart. If that's you, here are twelve practical tips guaranteed both to help get you unstuck and to keep you inspired.

First, a word of warning! Each of these twelve steps may seem easy to do; therefore, each one is easy *not* to do! If you stick with the template, your group will stick together far better. In fact, you can catapult most any traditional small group into a small circle of soul care by following this pattern. Don't just wing it; follow the plan!

1. Pray first and heed the prompts that come. As you pray and ponder over launching a soul care circle, pay attention to the friends who come to mind. Since the Lord directs our steps, He can also direct our thoughts and prompt certain people to cross our mental paths. Ask, "Lord, who might be open to embracing a refreshing connection with me and with others?"

2. Invite people. As you do, let them know that the invitation is for a certain number of months and not for the rest of their life! Groups typically cycle with seasons. Most groups shoot for the spring semester and the fall semester. Rarely will groups flourish during the holiday season or during the summer. Accept that and respect that.

3. Clarify the agenda. The most transformational groups are not primarily informational but relational. Yes, a

group study of the Bible is beneficial, but not unless it focuses on "applied theology." We're called not simply to be hearers of the Word, but doers of the Word! One way to structure a group is simply to discuss a chapter in a book like this one or a book of the New Testament or simply the message from the previous Sunday. Ask, "What might God be saying to you through this?"

4. Establish a refreshing routine. Everyone thrives in healthy routines personally, and the same is true relationally. Begin each session with a personal check-in. That is, ask everyone to simply share a word or phrase that sums up their current mood or situation. That word might be "I'm grateful," "I'm tired," "I'm confused," or "I'm at peace." Then each person says, "I'm all in!" To which the others in the group respond, "God bless you!" This is one of the regular rhythms that helps everyone assess their own feelings and better understand the feelings and circumstances of others.

5. "Take Two." The typical person is very uncomfortable with silence, especially in the presence of others. At most it's a matter of a few seconds before someone fills the void. In groups it's amazing what happens after purposely sitting in silence together for two full minutes. This isn't a waste of time! Silence allows the introverts to gather their thoughts, the extroverts to recalibrate their speech, and for everyone to be still in the presence of

God. So, determine to "take two" (i.e., two minutes of silence) at the beginning of every session.

6. Follow the 4 Ds template. Allowing everyone to share a *delight*, a *drain*, a *discovery* and a *determination for deeper connection* is highly engaging and bonding. Consistently following this pattern causes groups to coalesce quickly and to continue to grow closer. Everyone will soon look forward to this rhythm because they will not only discover fresh insights from others but often be surprised at what they hear themselves share! This verbalization opens easy and interesting conversation. Everyone is an expert on their own life experience and validated when others hear them process out loud.

7. Don't try to fix others; just listen. We need often to remind one another of the classic insight from esteemed psychiatrist Dr. Karl Menninger shared previously. Here it is again: "Listening is a magnetic and strange thing, a creative force. The friends who listen to us are the ones we move toward. When [we feel] we are listened to, it creates us, makes us unfold and expand."

8. Model and encourage affirmations. It's always good to affirm something someone has shared and even to summarize a particular point with the phrase "What I'm hearing you say is . . ." This simple approach is highly honoring.

9. Pray for one another. Most group prayers are awkward because most people don't know what to pray about. By contrast, praying out loud for the person next to you is both natural and highly personal. That's especially the case after you've just heard them share their 4 Ds. Prayer has been described as simply "keeping company with God." In every session everyone will be in "good company" with God and others!

10. Remember, confidentiality is key to candor. Regularly remind one another that personal things shared in the group will stay in the group. For example, if someone is struggling in their family, with their job, or with their health, they need to know that private things will remain private. No one should ever fear that they will be embarrassed later by something confidentially shared in a moment of concern or confession.

11. Keep a journal of insights. Brain studies document that we retain far more when we write things down. Encourage everyone to bring a journal to record some of their learnings from the group conversation each week. I strongly encourage everyone to make this a handwritten journal and not an electronic one. The tangible record of your sessions will soon become an inspiring and refreshing treasure trove!

12. Make hope a habit. Those who seek to serve as physicians of the soul must lead and love others with

the confidence that God isn't finished with any of us yet. We must never lose our grip on the reality of the resurrection. If God can raise the dead, there is nothing He cannot do. Those with the strongest hope in God will be the strongest leaders of God's people.

Leading and facilitating a soul care circle is a high privilege requiring careful and persistent direction. No one person needs to have all the answers. The circle gatherings are not Bible lessons but an experience of mutual learning. We learn as we listen, both to others and to ourselves. That being said, one person must assume the special role of insuring that the template is followed and that each member is heard.

If you want to go deeper, you must focus on fewer. Transformation happens best in circles, not in rows. We recommend that the circles be limited to four to seven individuals and that, once the circle bonds, additional members not be included. Groups take time to mature and to build trust. Consistently following these simple steps will encourage that to happen more quickly than you can imagine.

WHOM DO YOU TRUST?

Having led over forty retreats with this soul care template, I know that it not only works but that it produces transformational results! But you will need to trust the process.

We're all in the same boat right now, and the boat is called *Ruthless Trust*! I just reread the highlights of one of my favorite books with that very title. Author Brennan Manning shares the enlightening account of when, John Kavanaugh, brilliant ethicist and professor of philosophy, went to work with Mother Teresa at the House of the Dying in Calcutta. On their first morning of his three months of service she asked, "And what can I do for you?"

Kavanaugh simply asked her to pray for him.

"What do you want me to pray for?" she asked.

He humbly replied, "Pray that I have clarity."

She said firmly, "No, I will not do that."

When he asked her why, she said, "Clarity is the last thing you are clinging to and must let go of."

When Kavanaugh commented that she always seemed to have the clarity he longed for, she laughed and said, "I have never had clarity; what I have always had is trust. So I will pray that you trust God."[55]

Trusting that God loves you and that He is with you and for you is vital. However, it's also essential that we find a vital few of whom we could say the same thing!

Sure, you may have been hurt or betrayed in the past. You may feel overwhelmed with life stresses and overextended by unceasing demands. I get it—you're not making this up—life is tough.

But consider this, now is not forever! Might it be that some of the richest, most rewarding relationships you've ever had are still yet ahead? Stop procrastinating and start investing in others. The health of your soul is at stake!

REFLECTION QUESTIONS

What have you been procrastinating on?

Do you tend to lean into the future or fear it?

What inspires you about what may be next?

WHAT SEEDS ARE YOU PLANTING?

"O LORD, YOU ALONE ARE MY HOPE. I'VE TRUSTED YOU, O LORD, FROM CHILDHOOD. ...

NOW THAT I AM OLD AND GRAY, DO NOT ABANDON ME, O GOD. LET ME PROCLAIM YOUR POWER TO THIS NEW GENERATION, YOUR MIGHTY MIRACLES TO ALL WHO COME AFTER ME."

—PSALM 71:5, 18

You are writing your legacy now. Everyone will be remembered for something. How do you want to be remembered?

This is a timely question for me as I wrap up this book and begin the final chapter of my life.

There are two things for which I would like to be remembered.

I want to be remembered for investing in other people to the point that they flourish. I would love for it to be said of me, "His fruit grows on other people's trees."

I also want to be remembered as a man who lived *with* Jesus as well as *for* Him. After all, as much as we take pride in our to-do lists, the ultimate legacy is what we did *with* Jesus. It's a life lived in partnership, through the presence and power of the Holy Spirit. "And this is the secret: Christ lives in you. This gives you assurance of sharing his glory" (Colossians 1:27).

Our lasting legacy is not our performance *for* Christ, but our partnership *with* Christ and our position *in* Christ! There is only One who has lived a perfect life and He is the One who has promised to redeem all things and make all things new.

WHAT SEEDS ARE YOU PLANTING?

I love the story told in *The Man Who Planted Trees* by Jean Giono. The author tells of an encounter in the French Alps with a simple shepherd. Every night, the shepherd carefully sorted out a hundred perfect acorns to plant the next day.

Here's how Ken Gire summarized it in his book *Life as We Would Want It . . . Life as We Are Given It*:

At the time, because of careless deforestation, the mountains around Provence, France, were barren. Former villages were deserted because the springs and brooks had run dry. The wind blew furiously, unimpeded by foliage.

While mountain climbing, Giono came to a shepherd's hut, where he was invited to spend the night.

After dinner Giono watched the shepherd meticulously sort through a pile of acorns, discarding those that were cracked or undersized. When the shepherd had counted out one hundred perfect acorns, he stopped for the night and went to bed.

Giono learned that the fifty-five-year-old shepherd had been planting trees on the wild hillsides for over three years. He had planted one hundred thousand trees, twenty thousand of which had sprouted. Of those, he expected half to be eaten by rodents or die due to the elements, and the other half to live. . . .

The barren mountains around Provence, France, were reclaimed a seed at a time. It took years to sow them, and years to grow them. Little by little life returned. First the trees. Then the streams. And finally the villages, teeming with new life and the spirit of adventure.[56]

How did that transformation happen? Slowly and deliberately. It was the daily and faithful planting of acorns that eventually produced a stunning revitalization. It happened over time, not overnight.

We are all sowing seeds as we journey through life. What we do matters. If we keep sowing spiritual "seeds" and planting spiritual "trees" in faith, by God's grace we will help to change the landscape of our community, our country, and our world. But it all begins with changing the landscape of our own soul.

To leave a legacy, rather than to live merely for a résumé, we must all choose to live for something bigger than ourselves. Something more important than ourselves. Something that will last beyond ourselves.

While our timetable is temporal, God's timetable is eternal. Therefore, we thrive on the high-octane fuel of hope, trusting not in ourselves but in the Lover of our souls, the only One who can redeem all things.

Every day we must choose to plant seeds in hope, trusting God for the harvest yet to come, even if the harvest is long after we're gone. That's why I frequently pray, "Lord, help me to live for what will live on, with others who will live on!"

As a young man in ministry I was frequently disappointed with the lack of results I was seeing. When my parents came to South Carolina to visit us, I shared my frustration while on a rainy day car ride with my father. I'll never forget the moment when he quietly said something like this: "If you take care of the depth of your ministry, God will take care of the breadth of your ministry."

God used those wise words to lead me down a relational road. I had a lot to learn about being *with* the Lord and *with* other people. The application of that challenge for me required an increasing depth of relationships, both vertically with Christ and horizontally with the body of Christ.

Isn't it interesting that when Jesus chose the twelve apostles, as we're told in Mark 3:14 (NIV), He "appointed twelve that they might be with him." The words *with him* have always jumped off the page for me. Jesus is reminding us all that it's not just a matter of what you do in life or where you go, but who it is that is doing things and going places with you!

At the end of your days you will consider your greatest assets to be your relational ones!

IT'S NOT TOO SOON TO THINK ABOUT THE RELATIONAL LEGACY YOU WILL LEAVE

"I am going to die. By the time you read these lines, I may even be dead . . . I don't know when I will die. I just know I will. I am going to die, and so are you."

Those are the opening words in David Gibson's sobering book *Living Life Backward: How Ecclesiastes Teaches Us to Live in Light of the End.* He writes, "If you knew that death would happen tomorrow, how would you live today? That is the point of Ecclesiastes."[57]

Are you ready to die today?

That's the question that often grips me every morning. As Solomon said in Ecclesiastes 7:4, "A wise person thinks a lot about death."

When it comes to the length of our lives, neither you nor I have any guarantees. This could be the last thing I ever write or you ever read. If that's the case, ponder these words from *The Imitation of Christ* by Thomas a Kempis:

Happy is he that always hath the hour of his death before his eyes and daily prepareth himself to die . . .

When it is morning think thou mayest die before night and when evening comes dare not to promise thyself the next morning.

Be thou therefore always in readiness and so lead thy life so that death may never take thee unprepared.

When my father died at the age of eighty-three, his inbox was empty. Dad told me that he prayed every night with his palms open saying, "Lord, I'm ready to go any time you are ready to take me!" That's a bold prayer, and frankly, I'm not so sure I'm ready to pray it. I still have some immediate things that I want and hope to do.

I begin every day with a to-do list. I hope to live well until I die, with something significant to do. However, while I have several things I would like to do in the immediate category, I have nothing left to accomplish in the ultimate category.

Jesus has taken care of everything that is of ultimate importance. As I like to remind others, and most of all myself, the position of Savior has been taken. Therefore, if this is my last day, I can relax in His sovereignty.

People of faith, hope, and love will never be irrelevant.

The finest legacy anyone can leave is not an inheritance but a heritage. The ultimate mark of finishing well is not a big ministry, successful business, or best-selling book.

In other words, the finest legacy isn't anything that points people to us. Rather, it's a life of love that invests in other people, all the while pointing to the eternal One who is the Alpha and the Omega, the beginning and the end, the Lord over life and death.

An awareness of the temporariness of life is a gift of God that brings meaning to life. We are each called to invest and enjoy each day, compliments of God. This is a day we have never seen before and will never see again, and it just may be our last. That's not intended to prompt sadness but soberness and thoughtfulness.

How will you invest your remaining days and years?

What relationships will you pour yourself into?

Will you perform *for* God—or partner *with* Him?

What legacy will you leave?

May the God of hope fill you with all joy and peace as you
trust in him, so that you may overflow with hope by the
power of the Holy Spirit.
(Romans 15:13 NIV).

By God's grace may you be filled to overflowing with hope, believing that the best is always yet to be!

ABOUT THE AUTHOR

Alan Ahlgrim has spent over half his life in Colorado. He is the father of three married children and six grandchildren. He and his wife for life, Linda, thoroughly enjoy an active life, hiking, kayaking, biking, and walking together with their Australian Labradoodle, Molly Brown, the Dog of Renown! Alan served twenty-nine years as the founding pastor of Rocky Mountain Christian Church in Colorado, as well as helped to energize a national resurgence of church planting. He is now leveraging the agony and ecstasy of fifty years of ministry in his encore role as founder and chief soul care officer of Covenant Connections.

Alan invests heavily in the hard work of heart work, helping other leaders serve well and finish well by connecting them in soul-enriching covenant groups. These small, in-depth communities are transformational and produce remarkable renewal and resilience. For more information visit covenantconnections.life.

NOTES

1   Oswald Chambers, *My Utmost for His Highest*, updated edition, December 15 (Grand Rapids, MI: Oswald Chambers Publications in affiliation with Our Daily Bread Ministries, 1935; 1992), 350.

2   Mark Buchanan, *Hidden in Plain Sight: The Secret of More* (Nashville, TN: Thomas Nelson, 2012), 3.

3   Oswald Chambers, *My Utmost for His Highest*, updated edition, May 1 (Grand Rapids, MI: Oswald Chambers Publications in affiliation with Our Daily Bread Ministries, 1935; 1992), 122.

4   Henri Nouwen, *The Wounded Healer: Ministry in Contemporary Society* (New York: Image Books/Doubleday, 1972), 42–43, 78.

5   Marvin Olasky, "Why so many criminals? How modern justice system practices miss the heart of the problem," World magazine, October 9, 2017, https://wng.org/articles/why-so-many-criminals-1620611987.

6   Angela Lu Fulton, "Shut in and shut out," World magazine November 11, 2017, https://wng.org/articles/shut-in-and-shut-out-1620597080.

7   Charity Byers and John Walker, *Unhindered: Aligning the Story of Your Heart* (Calabasas, CA: Avail Press, 2020), 56.

8   Henri Nouwen, *The Wounded Healer: Ministry in Contemporary Society* (New York: Image Books/Doubleday, 1972), 42–43.

9   Brennan Manning, *Ruthless Trust: The Ragamuffin's Path to God* (New York: HarperCollins, 2000), 5.

10 Doc Childre and Howard Martin, with Donna Beech, *The HeartMath Solution: The Institute of HeartMath's Revolutionary Program for Engaging the Power of the Heart's Intelligence* (New York: HarperCollins, 1999), 23.

11 Doc Childre and Howard Martin, with Donna Beech, *The HeartMath Solution: The Institute of HeartMath's Revolutionary Program for Engaging the Power of the Heart's Intelligence* (New York: HarperCollins, 1999), 55.

12 John Ortburg, *Soul Keeping: Caring for the Most Important Part of You* (Grand Rapids: Zondervan, 2014).

13 Ibid.

14 Joseph Myers, *The Search to Belong: Rethinking Intimacy, Community, and Small Groups* (Grand Rapids, MI: Zondervan, 2003), 5, 20, 151.

15 Tim Keller with Kathy Keller, *God's Wisdom for Navigating Life: A Year of Daily Devotions in the Book of Proverbs* (New York: Viking, 2017), 164.

16 Gordon MacDonald, *Renewing Your Spiritual Passion* (Nashville: Thomas Nelson, 1986), 71–88.

17 Paul Tournier, *A Place for You: Psychology and Religion* (City: Publisher, Year), 9.

18 Brené Brown, *The Gifts of Imperfection: Let Go of Who You Think You're Supposed to Be and Embrace Who You Are* (Center City, MN: Hazelden, 2010), 12.

19 Robert Putnam, Bowling Alone: The Collapse and Revival of American Community (New York: Simon and Schuster, 2001).

20   Wes Beavis, *Let's Talk About Ministry Burnout: A Proven Research-based Approach to the Wellbeing of Pastors* (Powerborn Publishing).

21   Sean Morgan, "Aaron Brockett Talks Building Trust and Bringing Change Through Transition," *Leaders in Living Rooms*, podcast, November 14, 2019.

22   David Benner, *Sacred Companions: The Gift of Spiritual Friendship & Direction* (Downers Grove, IL: InterVarsity Press, 2002).

23   David Benner, *Sacred Companions*.

24   M. Robert Mulholland, *Invitation to a Journey: A Road Map for Spiritual Formation* (Downers Grove, IL: InterVarsity Press, 1993), 16.

25   John Ortberg, *The Life You've Always Wanted: Spiritual Disciplines for Ordinary People* (Grand Rapids, MI: Zondervan, 1997, 2002), 20.

26   Chip Heath and Dan Heath, *The Power of Moments: Why Certain Experiences Have Extraordinary Impact* (New York: Simon & Schuster, 2017), 243–46.

27   Ian Morgan Cron, *The Road Back to You: An Enneagram Journey to Self-Discovery* (Downers Grove, IL: InterVarsity Press, 2016), 137.

28   Tyler Zach, *The Gospel for Achievers: A 40-Day Devotional for Driven, Successful Go-Getters (Enneagram 3)* (self-pub., 2020), 82.

29   Doc Childre and Howard Martin, with Donna Beech, *The HeartMath Solution: The Institute of HeartMath's Revolutionary Program for Engaging the Power of the Heart's Intelligence* (New York: HarperCollins, 1999), 23, 55.

30 Dan Britton, Jimmy Page, and Jon Gordon, *One Word That Will Change Your Life* (Hoboken, NJ: John Wiley & Sons, 2013), 6, 14–23.

31 Bob Buford, *Finishing Well: The Adventure of Life Beyond Halftime* (Grand Rapids, MI: Zondervan, 2004), 123–24.

32 Randy Alcorn, "Believer's Judgment of Works," Eternal Perspective Ministries, January 1, 1994, https://www.epm.org/resources/1994/Jan/1/believers-judgment-works/.

33 Michael John Cusick, *Surfing for God: Discovering the Divine Desire Beneath Sexual Struggle* (Nashville, TN: Thomas Nelson, 2012), 8.

34 C.S. Lewis, *Mere Christianity* (New York: Macmillan, 1952), 94–95.

35 C.S. Lewis, *A Year with C.S. Lewis: Daily Readings from His Classic Works*, Patricia S. Klein, ed., June 29 (San Francisco: HarperCollins, 2003), 197.

36 Henri Nouwen, *The Way of the Heart: Connecting with God Through Prayer, Wisdom, and Silence* (New York: Ballantine Books, 2003), 16.

37 C.S. Lewis, *Mere Christianity* (New York: Macmillan, 1952), 81.

38 R. Paul Stevens and Clive Lim, *Money Matters: Faith, Life, and Wealth* (Grand Rapids, MI: William B. Eerdmans, 2021).

39 Marjorie Thompson, *Soul Feast: An Invitation to the Christian Spiritual Life* (City: Publisher, Year), 69.

40 John Ortberg, *Soul Keeping: Caring for the Most Important Part of You* (Grand Rapids, MI: Zondervan, 2014), 32.

41   Tim Hansel, *You Gotta Keep Dancin'* David C. Cook
     Publishing Company, Elgin, Illinois 1985), 54.

42   Paul David Tripp, February 4, *New Morning Mercies: A Daily
     Gospel Devotional* (Wheaton, IL: Crossway, 2014).

43   D. Martyn Lloyd-Jones, *Spiritual Depression: Its Causes and
     Its Cure* (Grand Rapids, MI: William B. Eerdmans, 1972),
     20–21.

44   Bessel van der Kolk, *The Body Keeps the Score: Brain, Mind,
     and Body in the Healing of Trauma* (New York: Penguin,
     2014), 11.

45   David Brooks, "The Summoned Life," *The New York Times*,
     August 2, 2010.

46   John Stott, *The Radical Disciple: Some Neglected Aspects of
     Our Calling* (Downers Grove, IL: InterVarsity Press), 13.

47   John Baillie, *A Diary of Private Prayer* (New York: Scribner,
     1949), 115.

48   Mark Batterson, *In a Pit with a Lion on a Snowy Day: How
     to Survive and Thrive When Opportunity Roars* (New York:
     Multnomah, 2006), 69–70.

49   Maria Konnikova, "What's Lost as Handwriting Fades," *New
     York Times*, June 2, 2014.

50   Henry Cloud, *Necessary Endings: The Employees, Businesses,
     and Relationships That All of Us Have to Give Up in Order to
     Move Forward* (New York: HarperCollins, 2010), 6–8.

51   Bob Russell and Bryan Bucker, *Transition Plan* (Louisville,
     KY: Ministers Label, 2010).

52   Jeffrey Sennefeld, *The Heroes Farewell: What Happens When
     CEOs Retire?* (New York: Oxford University Press, 1988).

53   Bob Buford, *Finishing Well: The Adventure of Life Beyond Halftime* (Grand Rapids, MI: Zondervan, 2004), 123–24.

54   Tim Keller with Kathy Keller, *God's Wisdom for Navigating Life: A Year of Daily Devotions in the Book of Proverbs*, May 27 (New York: Viking, 2017), 147.

55   Brennan Manning, *Ruthless Trust: Trust: The Ragamuffin's Path to God* (New York: HarperCollins, 2000), 5.

56   Ken Gire, *Life as We Would Want It . . . Life as We Are Given It* (Nashville, TN: W Publishing Group, 2006), 79–82.

57   David Gibson, *Living Life Backward: How Ecclesiastes Teaches Us to Live in Light of the End* (Wheaton, IL: Crossway, 2017), 11.